flaminio gundy

Prague
The capital of white magic

Prague
The capital of white magic

by Flaminio Gundy

All rights reserved.
No part of this book may be used or reproduced in any manner without written permission of the publishers.

Copyright © 2019 by Flaminio Gundy

Kindle Direct Publishing, USA, 2019

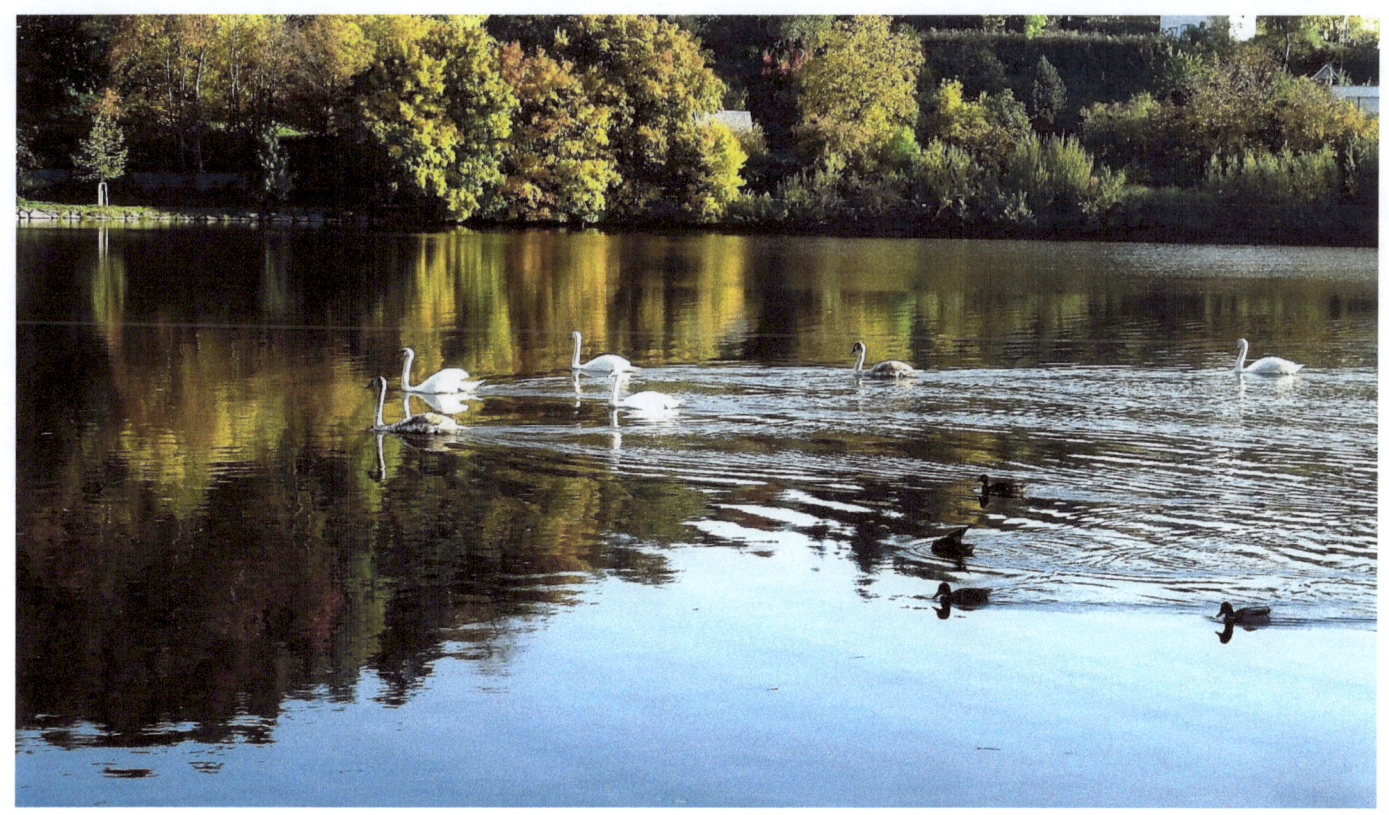

Bramborová Polévka, *potato soup*. Soak the dried porcini mushrooms for an hour and cut the vegetables (potatoes, carrot, celeriac and leek) into small pieces. Boil the vegetable stock and add all the vegetables, cumin, marjoram and cook for 30 minutes. Peel and finely chop the onion and garlic and brown them in butter. Put the flour and mix well. Pour the mixture into the soup and incorporate it well into the other ingredients. Season with salt and cook for 10 minutes. Mix the yogurt and cream together with an egg yolk and add them to the soup. Remove from heat, add parsley and serve.

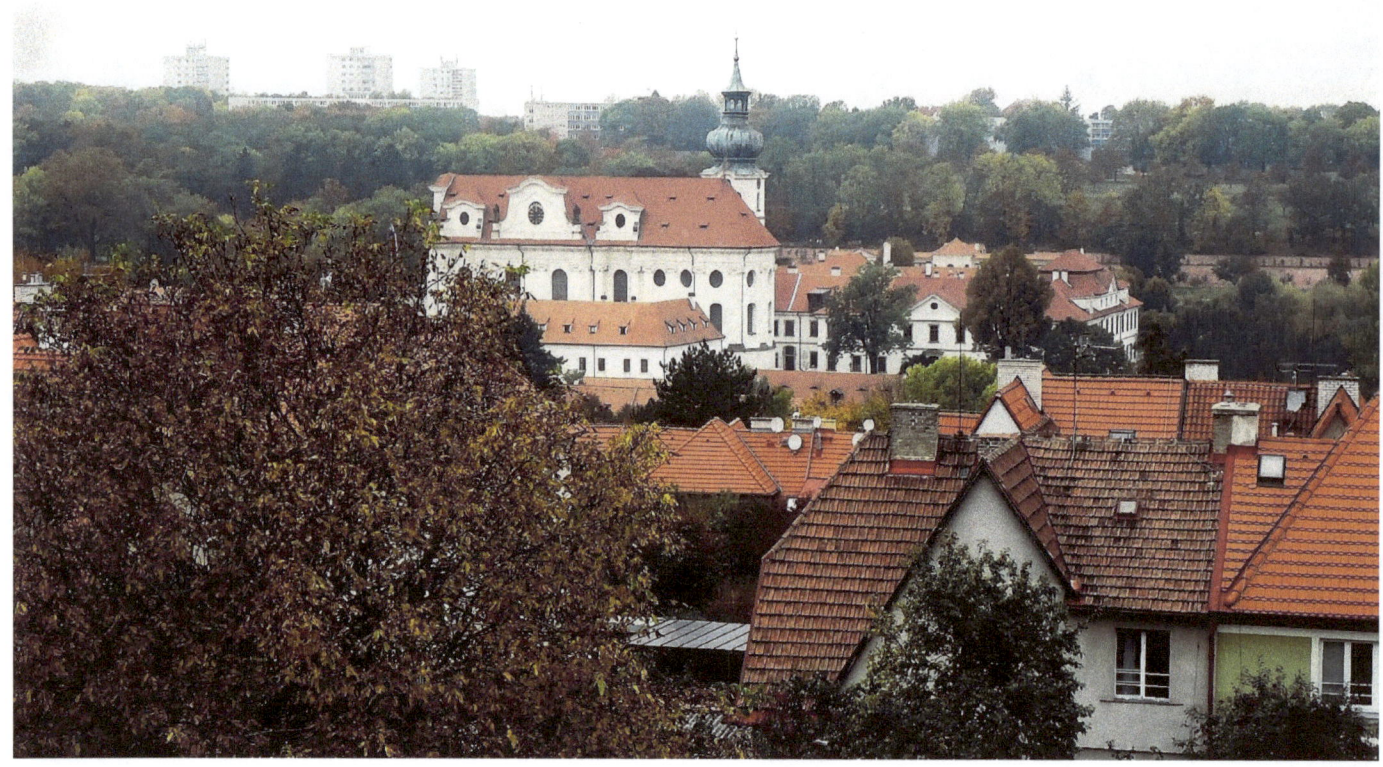

Čačkova Polévka s pàrky, *soup with lentils and sausages*. Fry the celery with the carrot in the butter, add the rinsed lentils (do not dip them in advance), pour the broth and cook. After about fifteen minutes, add the grated garlic, diced peeled potatoes and cook until tender. Then add the sliced sausages in small wheels, thicken the soup with the roux and mix well. Season the soup to taste with salt, pepper, vinegar and celery leaves (or parsley).

Roux is a compound of French origin which acts as a binding or thickening base for sauces, velvets and soups, obtained by mixing a part of flour with a portion of equal weight of melted butter, preferably clarified, or other type of fat.

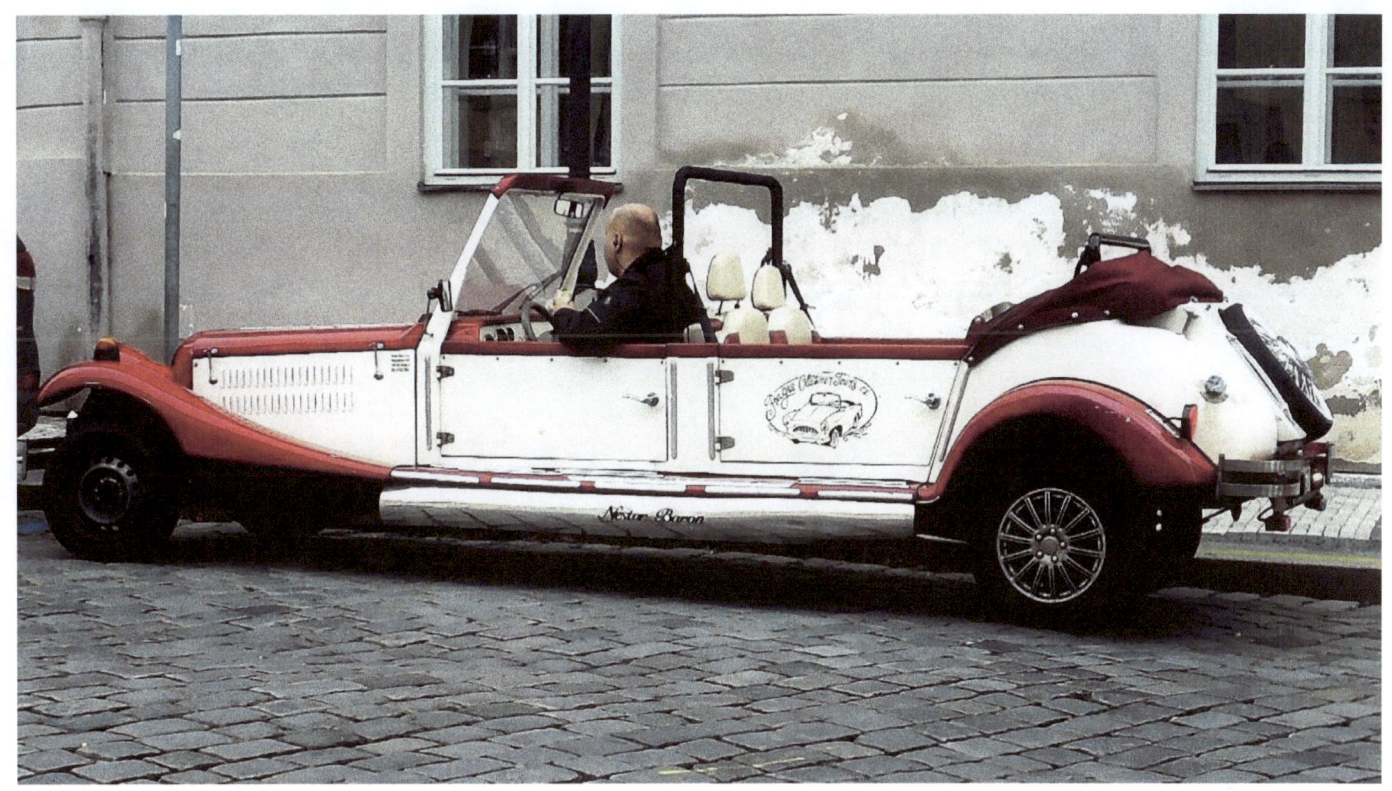

Česneková Polévka, *garlic soup*. Cut the bread into cubes and fry it in lard. Cut the peeled potatoes into cubes of about one cm, rinse them and put them in water, add salt, pepper, cumin, marjoram, strong broth, lard and cook. When the potatoes are almost soft, boil the egg in the soup and cook over a low heat. Finally add the garlic in the soup and season. Put the toasted bread in the garlic soup on the plate and serve.

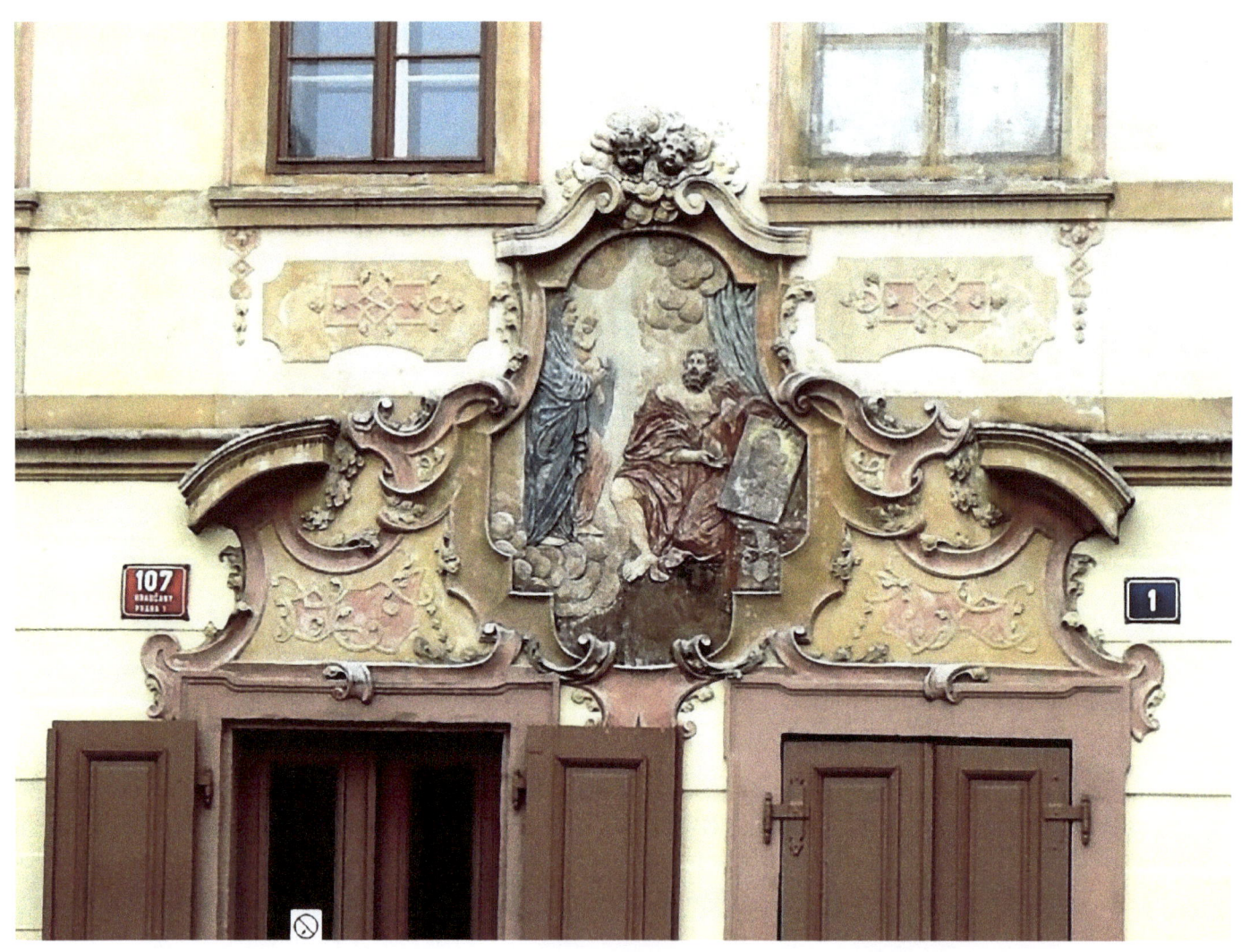

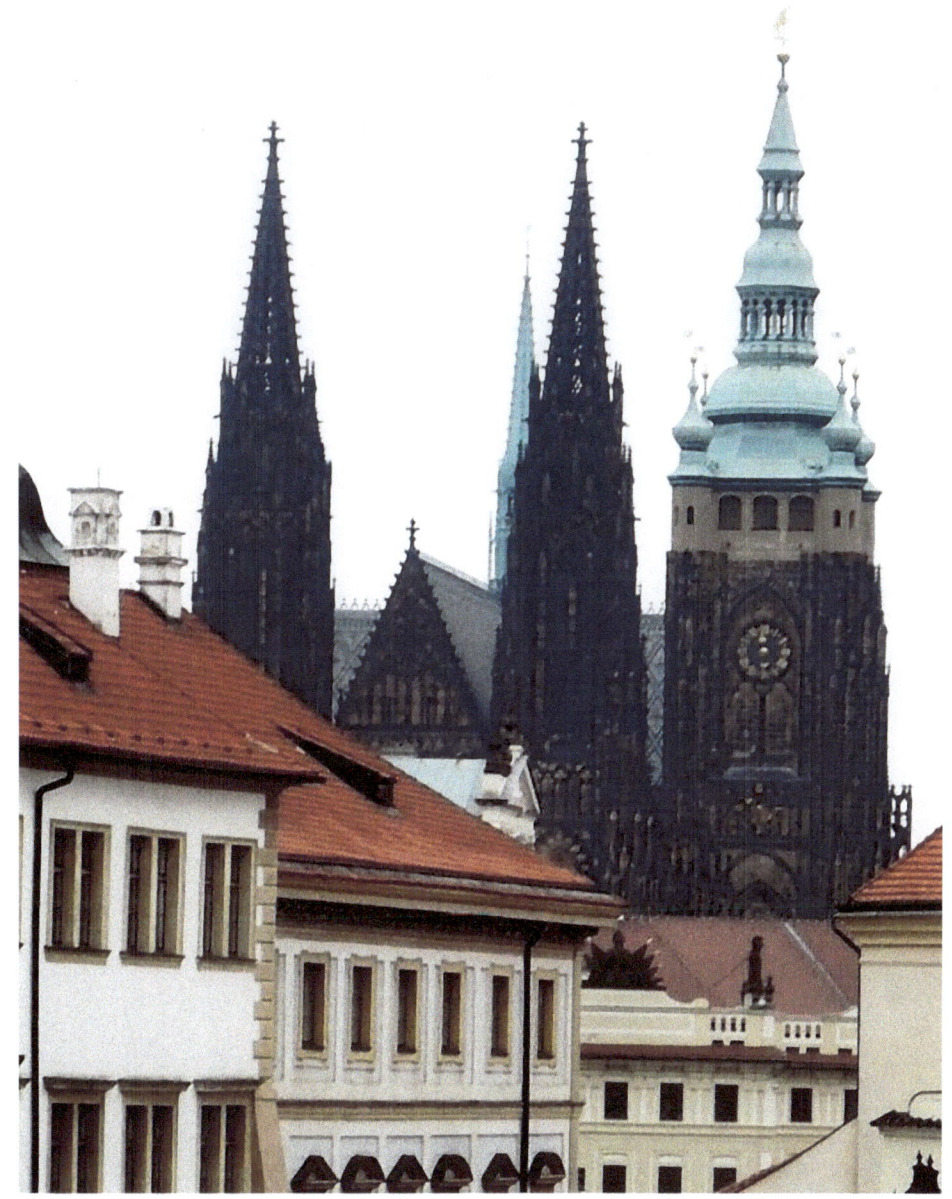

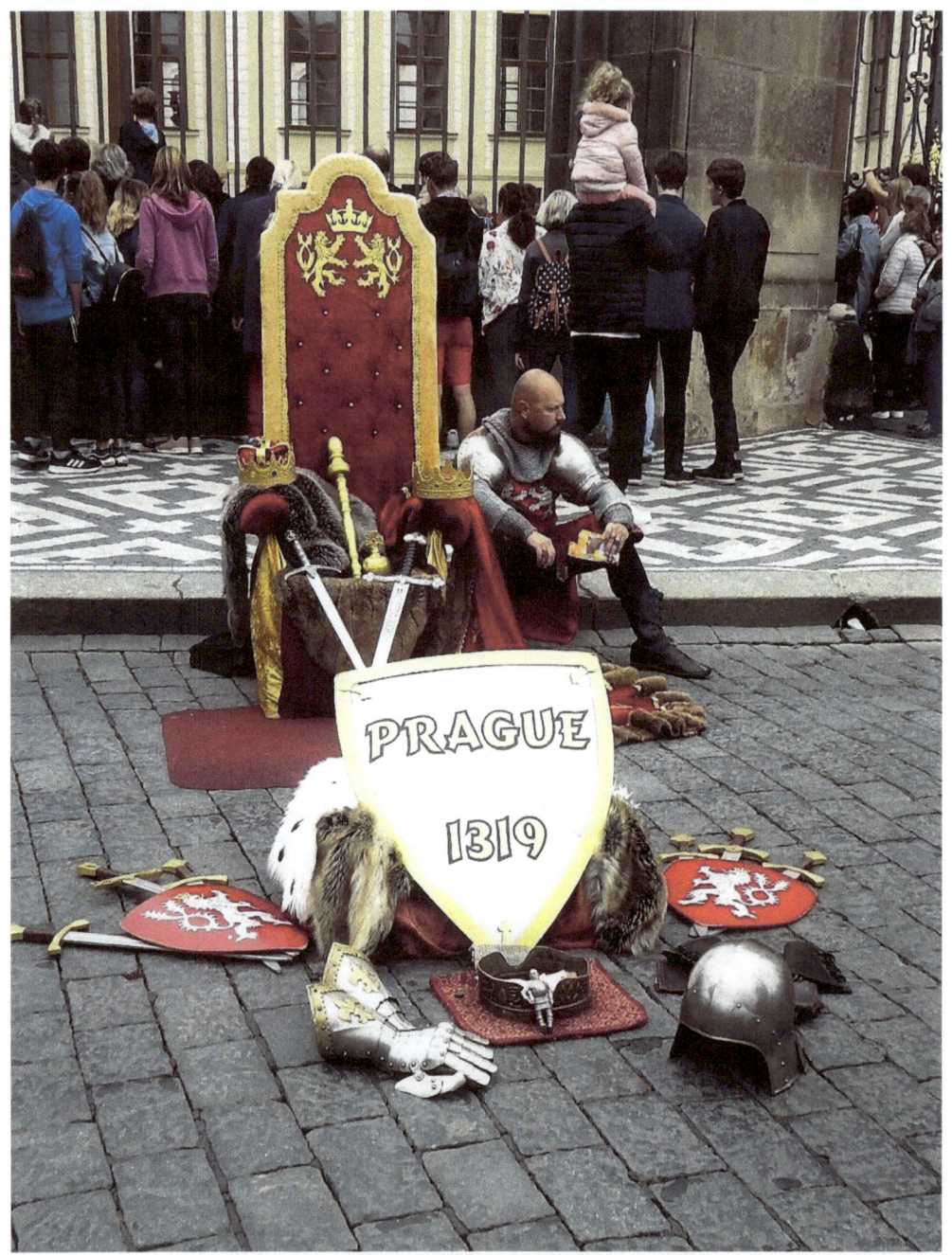

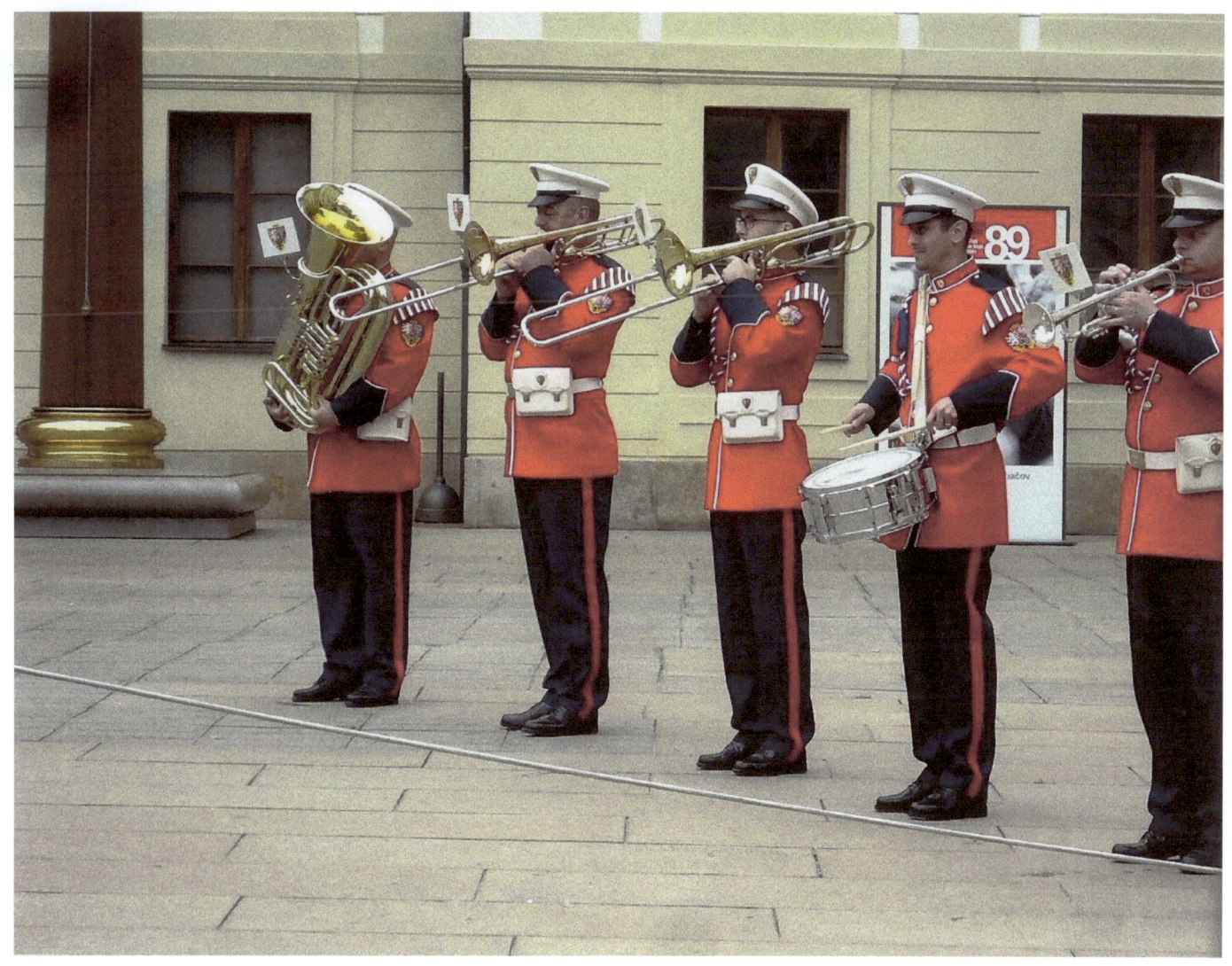

Koprová polévka, *dill soup made with sour milk*. Cut six potatoes into cubes, add a little water and add salt. When they are soft, add a liter of milk. Mix the flour in the cream to thicken it and pour it into the soup, stirring and let it simmer. Finally, add a sliced boiled egg and dill to the soup. Season with vinegar or lemon and soften with a teaspoon of butter.

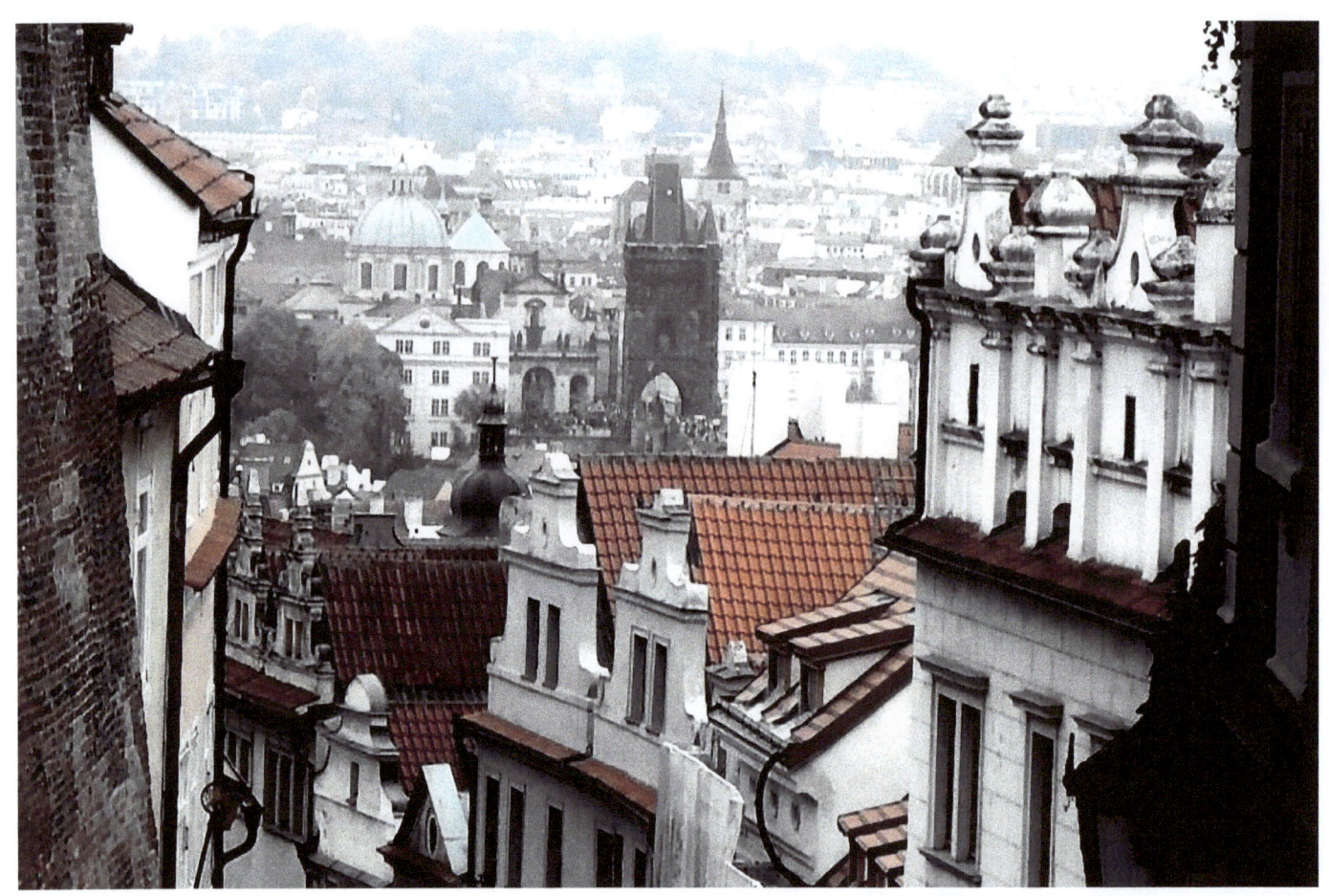

Hovězí polévka s játrovými knedlíčky, *beef soup with liver dumplings*. Wash the meat (shank and ribs of beef) in cold water, cut it into large pieces, put it in a pot, pour a few liters of cold water, bring it to a boil slowly and when the foam goes up on the surface and forms a thin layer, remove it with a spoon. The broth must remain clear. Reduce the heat to a minimum, add salt and pepper, half an onion with peel, celery and parsley, then simmer. Meanwhile, clean the vegetables (carrot, parsley, other celery, leek, cabbage, kohlrabi) and the mushrooms, cut them into thin slices and brown them in a large, deep pan on a warm lard. Add the chopped and sliced liver of chicken or pork and roast it on all sides for about 5 minutes. Pour the fat from the pan and add its contents to the broth and ferment it for 2-3 hours on a very delicate flame.

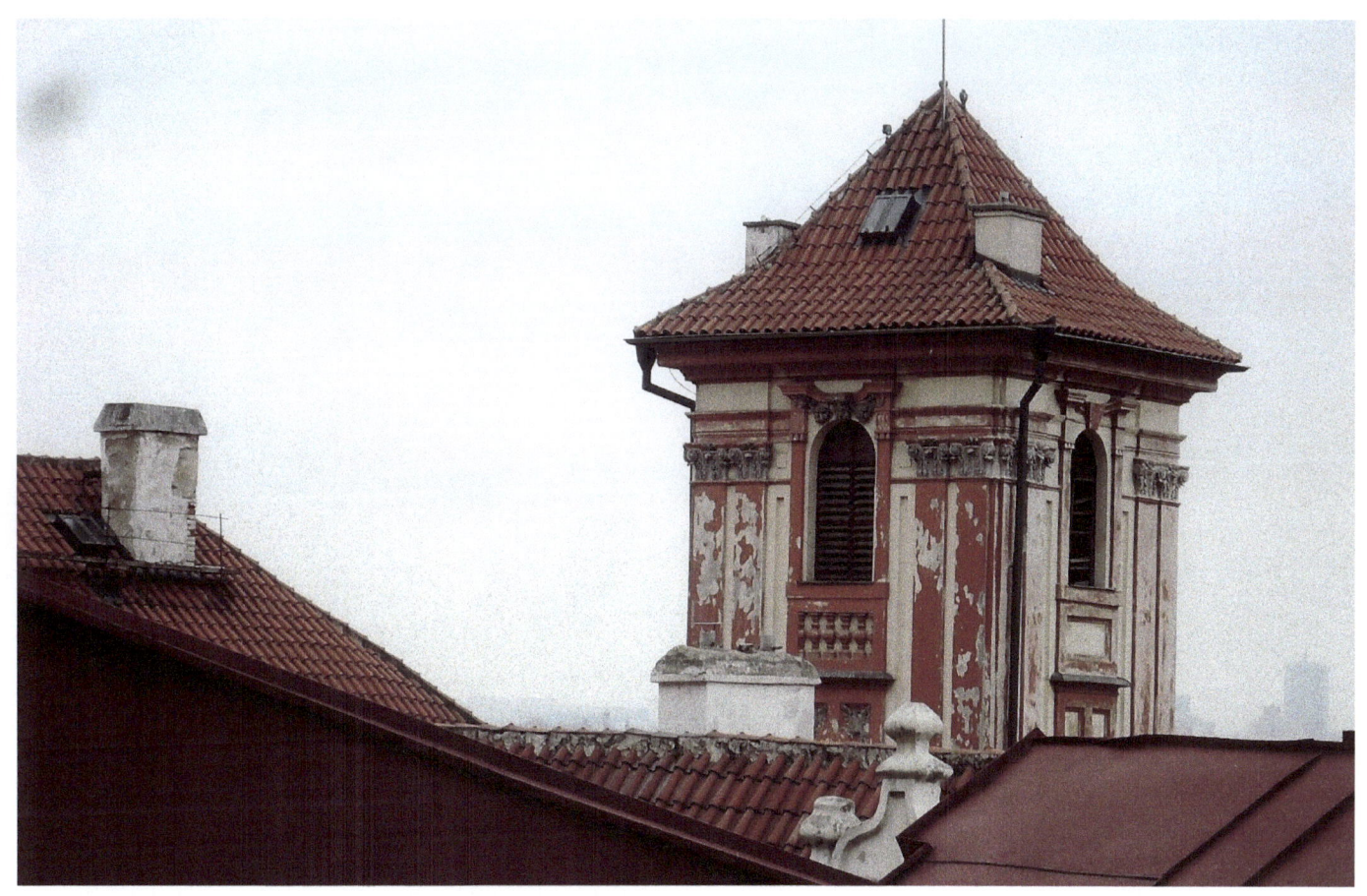

Remove the cooked meat and liver, cut them into pieces, collect the fat from the broth and strain through a fine sieve. Put the tagliatelle, the gnocchi and, if you want, the vegetables chopped in the broth. Let it heat and serve garnished with the remaining chives, parsley and lovage.
Liver dumplings. Wash the pork liver and chicken breast together with onion and garlic, add an egg, marjoram, chopped cumin, salt, pepper and stir. If necessary, thicken with breadcrumbs. Use a spoon to shape small dumplings and cook in the soup for about 5 minutes.

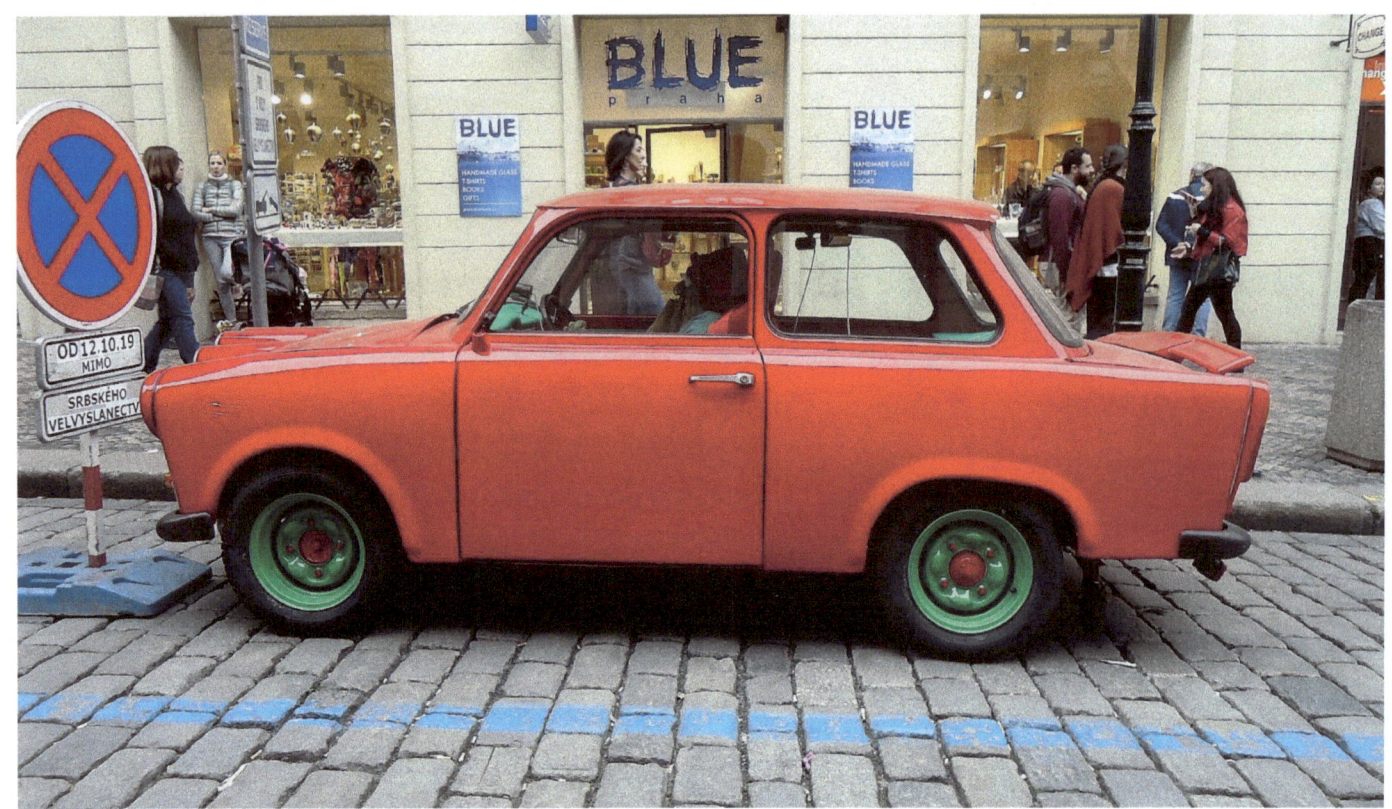

Kuřecí polévka s nudlemi, *chicken soup*. Put the chicken meat in a pan, pour cold water, add salt, allspice, pepper and cook until the meat is tender, continuously collecting the foam that forms on the surface during cooking. Pour the broth without the meat in a clean pan and bring it to a boil. Clean the carrot, parsley and celery, cut them into strips and cook them in the broth. Add the peeled onion and sliced garlic and cook until the vegetables are tender. Put the noodles in the soup, cook them for about 3 minutes, then put the soup out of the heat. Cut the meat into pieces, put it back in the soup, season with salt and sprinkle with parsley.

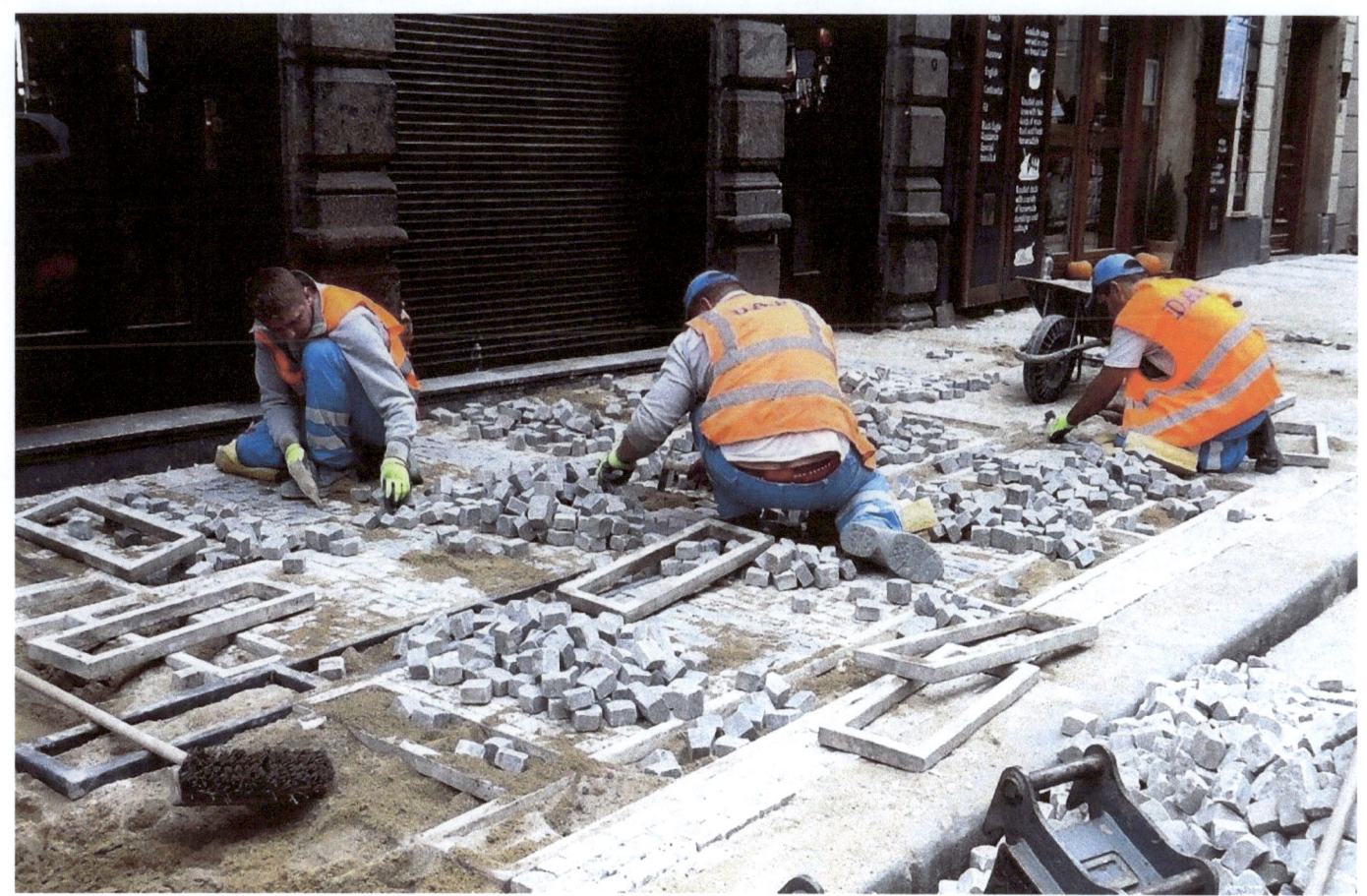

Zelná polévka, *sauerkraut soup*. Pour water into a pot, add a broth of strong meat and boil it. Add the drained and sliced cabbage and cook until tender. Then add the peeled and diced potatoes, season with salt, add the cumin and let it boil. Slice the finely chopped onion on a hot lard, sprinkle with flour and prepare a light roux. Dilute it with a portion of broth, pour it into the soup, stir and continue stirring until the potatoes are tender. Finally add the cream mixed with a little flour. Season the soup with vinegar and sprinkle with chopped parsley while serving.

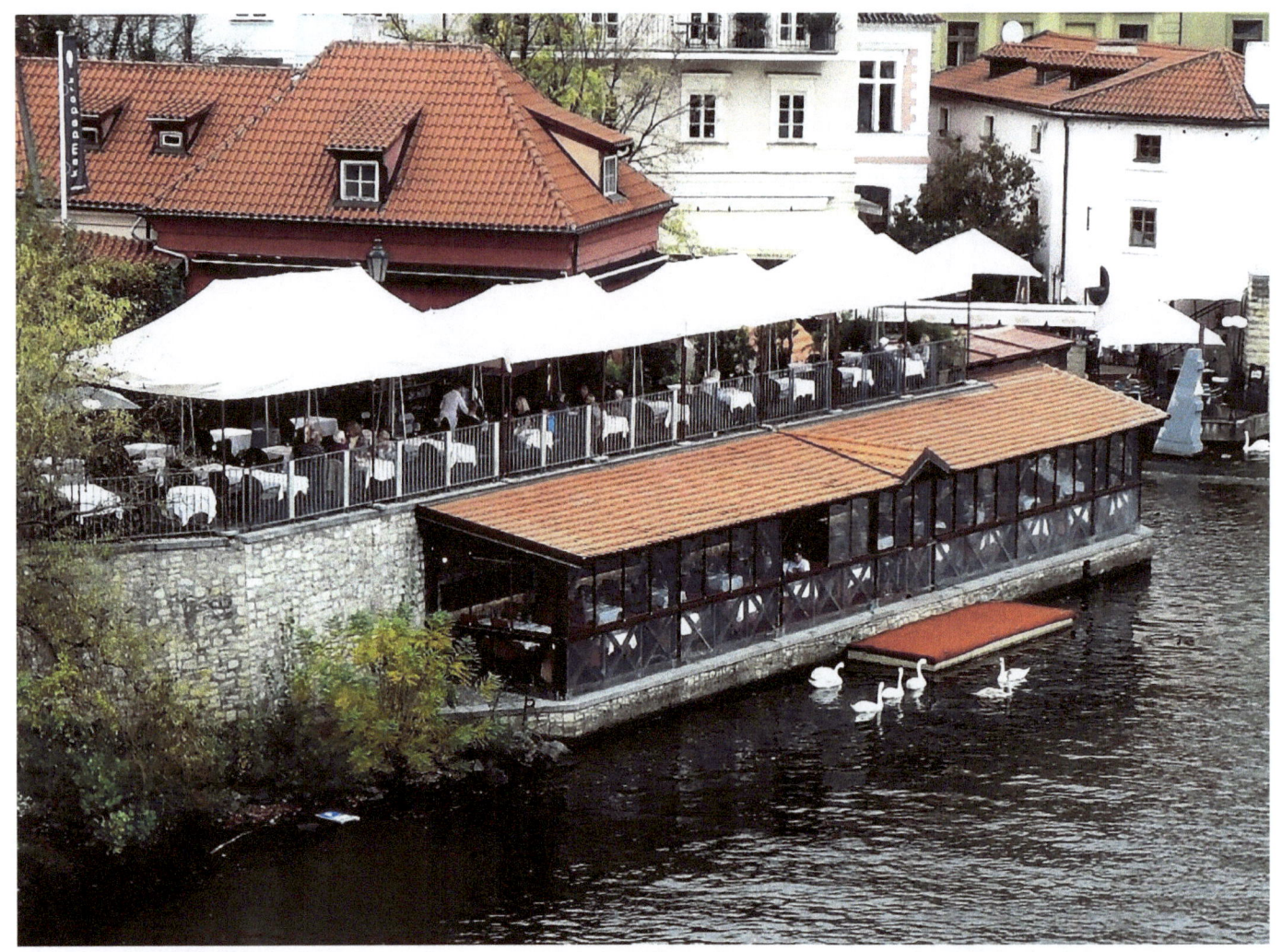

Bohemian gulas, *meat stew always accompanied by knedikly*. Brown a chopped onion in a veil of oil. In another pan, brown the diced lean beef in oil and sprinkle the mixture with two tablespoons of flour, turning the pieces of meat well. Add the browned onions and the broth dissolving any lumps. Add the paprika, the peeled tomatoes cut into small pieces and a pinch of salt. Boil with lid on low heat for about two and a half hours.

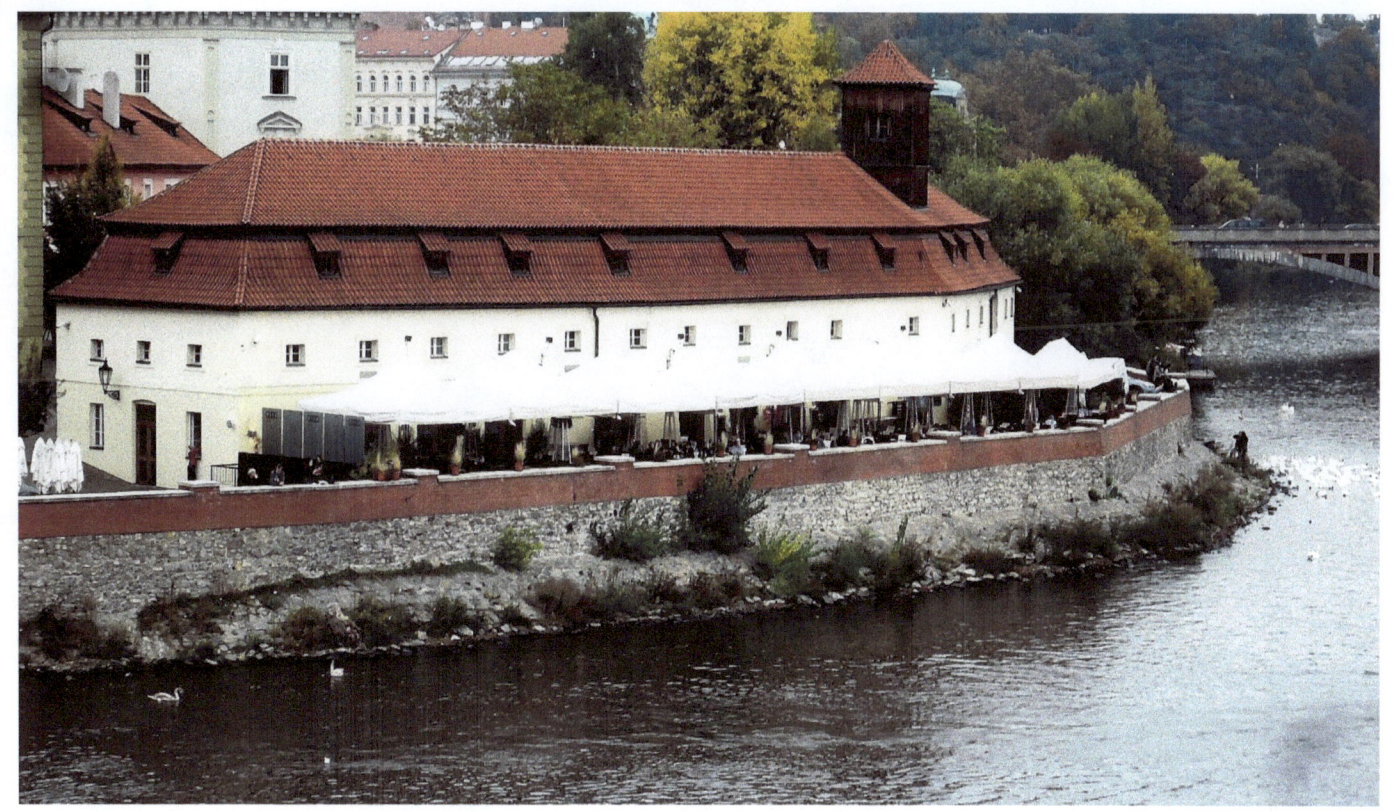

knedikly, *bread dumplings*. Melt half a fresh yeast cube in warm milk and knead it together with the flour and the whole egg. Add the salt and continue to knead. Add the crumbs of stale bread and knead for about ten minutes, then let it rest until the dough is doubled in size. Roll the dough and wrap it in a cotton cloth (you can also split it in two), not too tight, close it at the ends and wait half an hour. Bring the water to a boil in a saucepan and gently lay the sausage. After 15 minutes turn it over and continue cooking for another 15 min. Remove it from the pan and let it evaporate. Gently cut (better with a thread) and serve with the goulash.

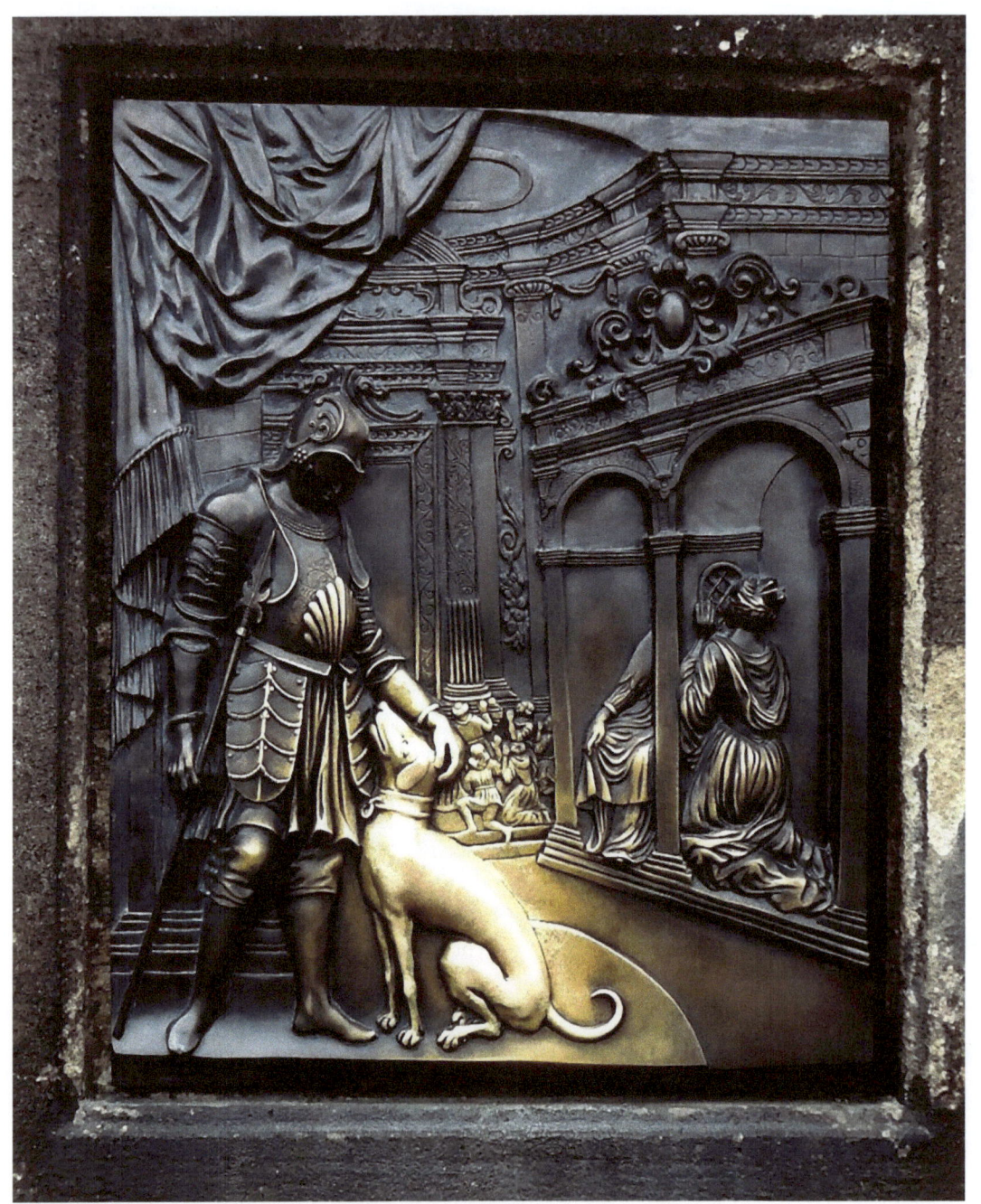

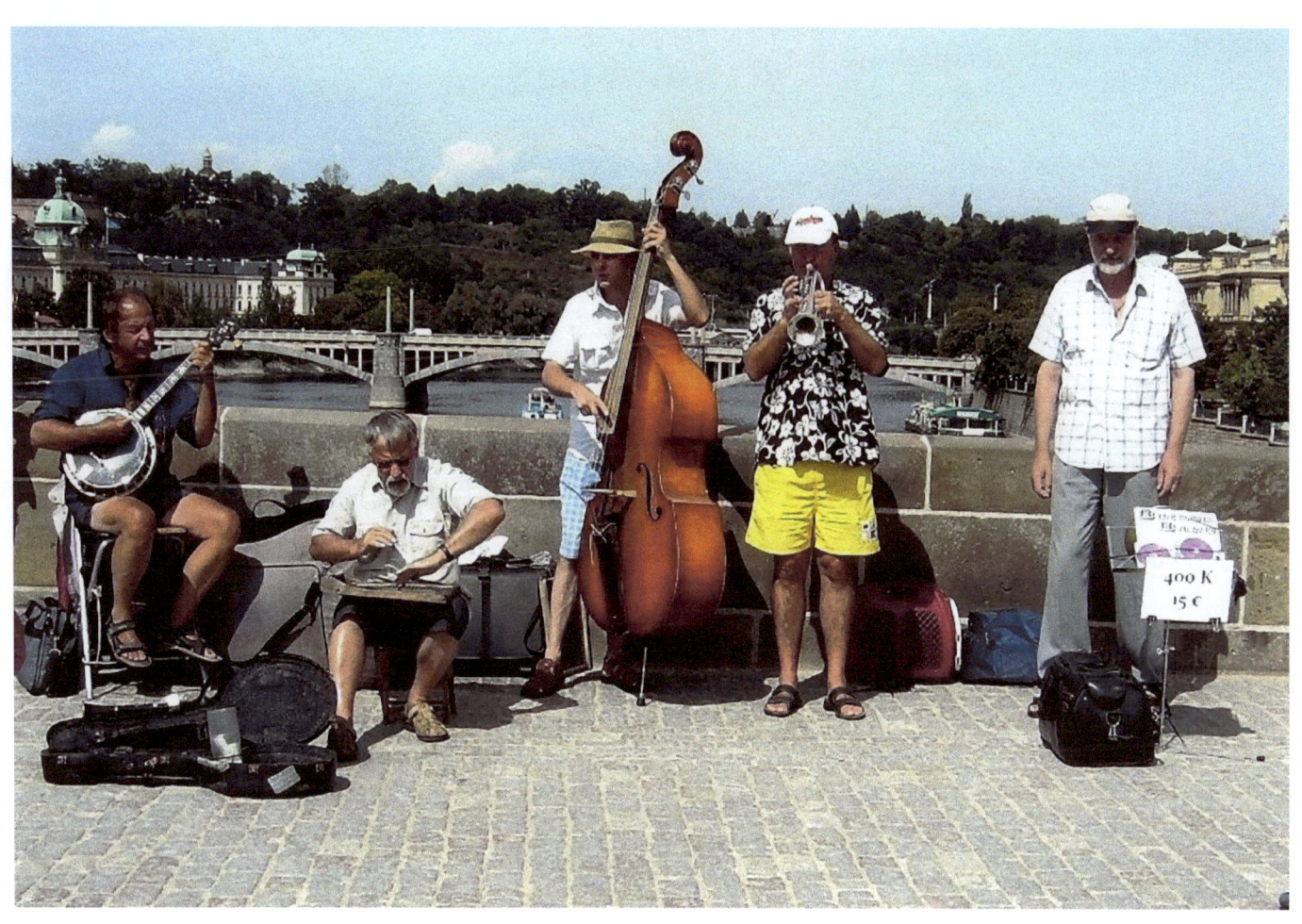

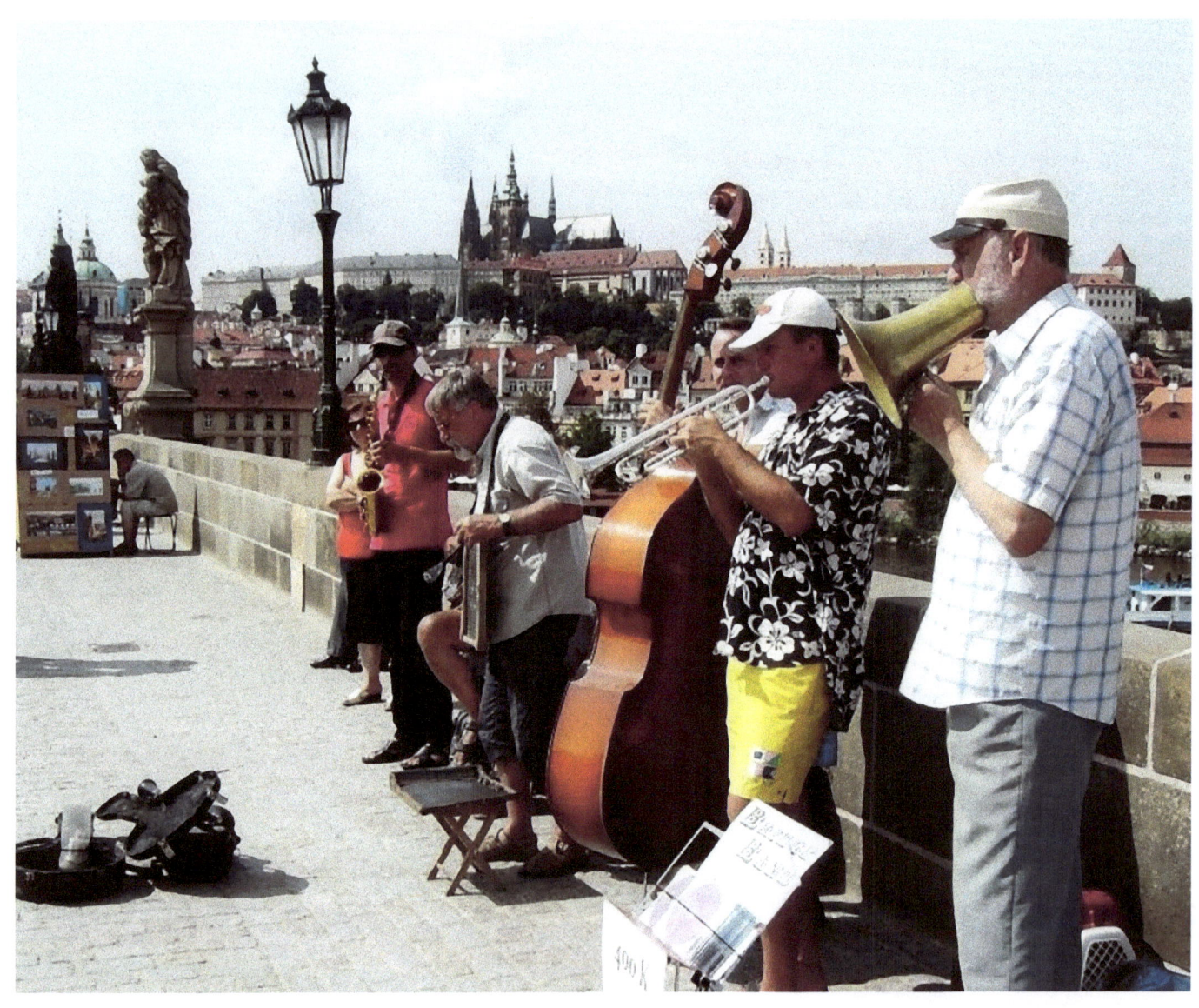

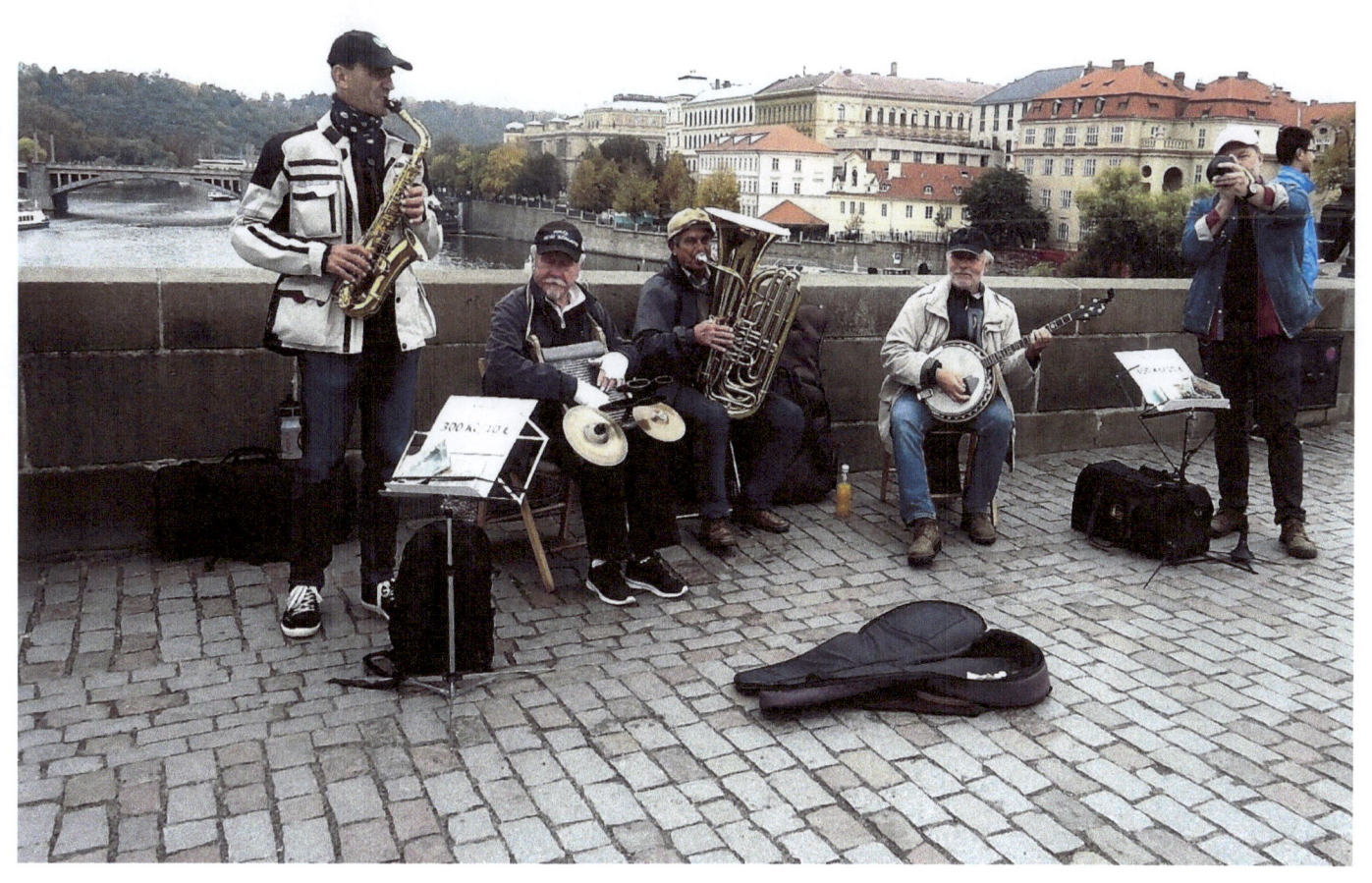

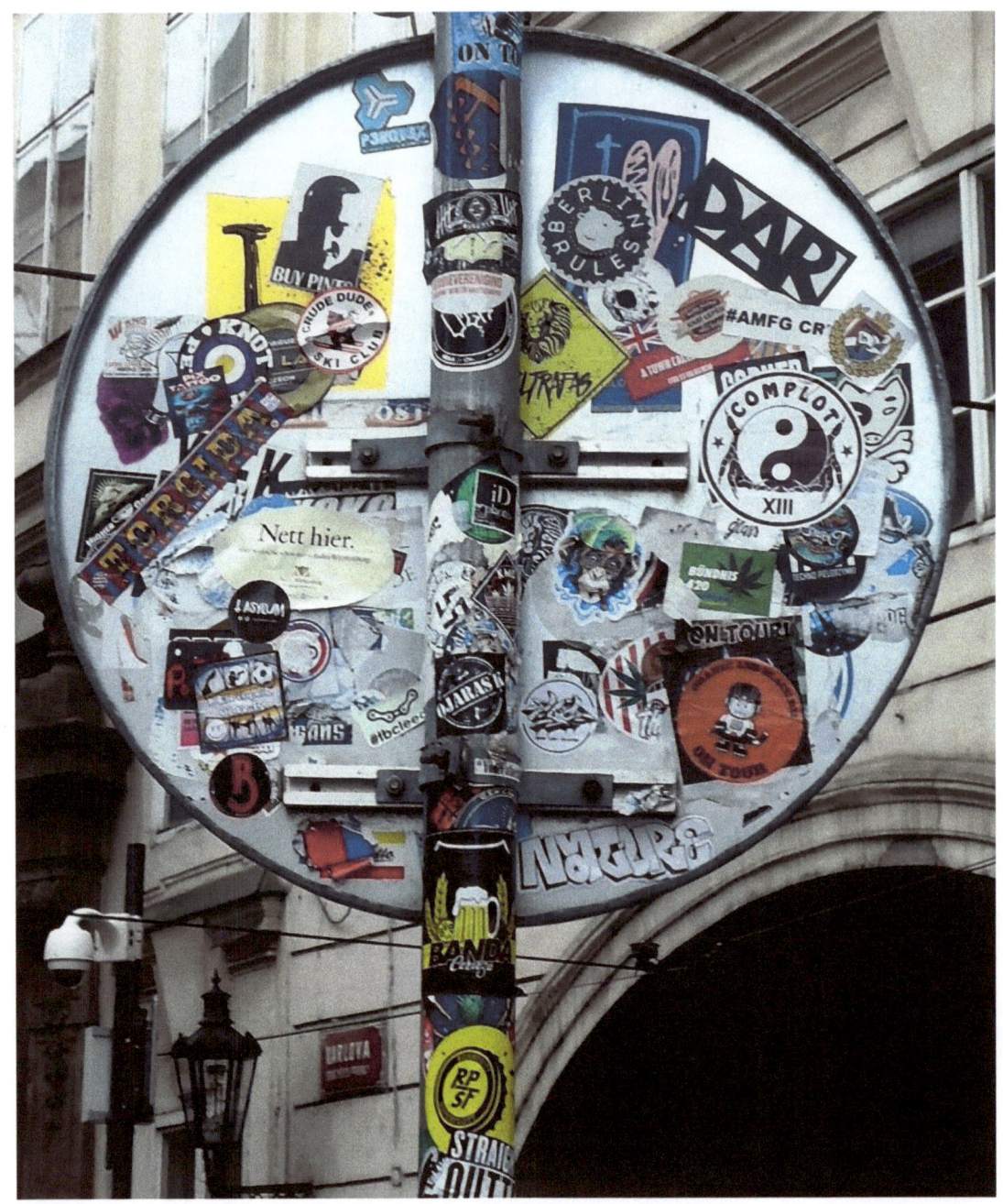

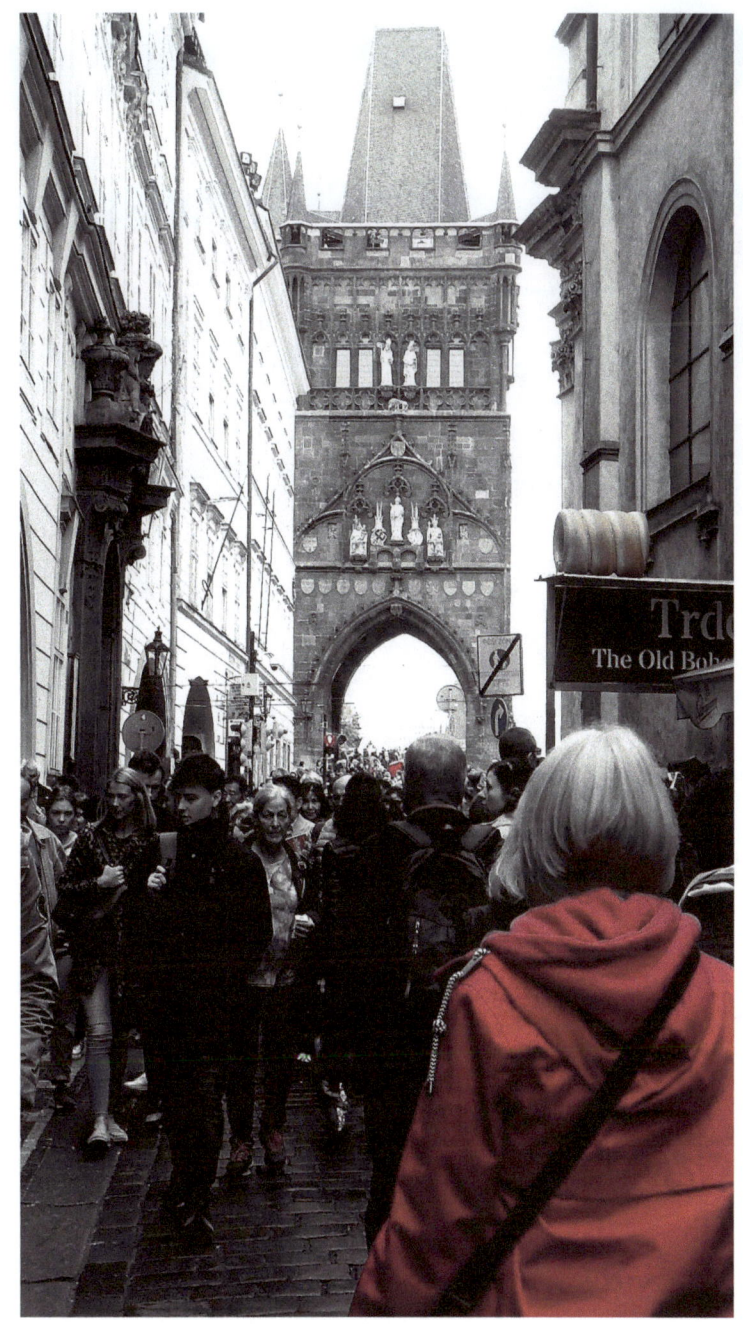

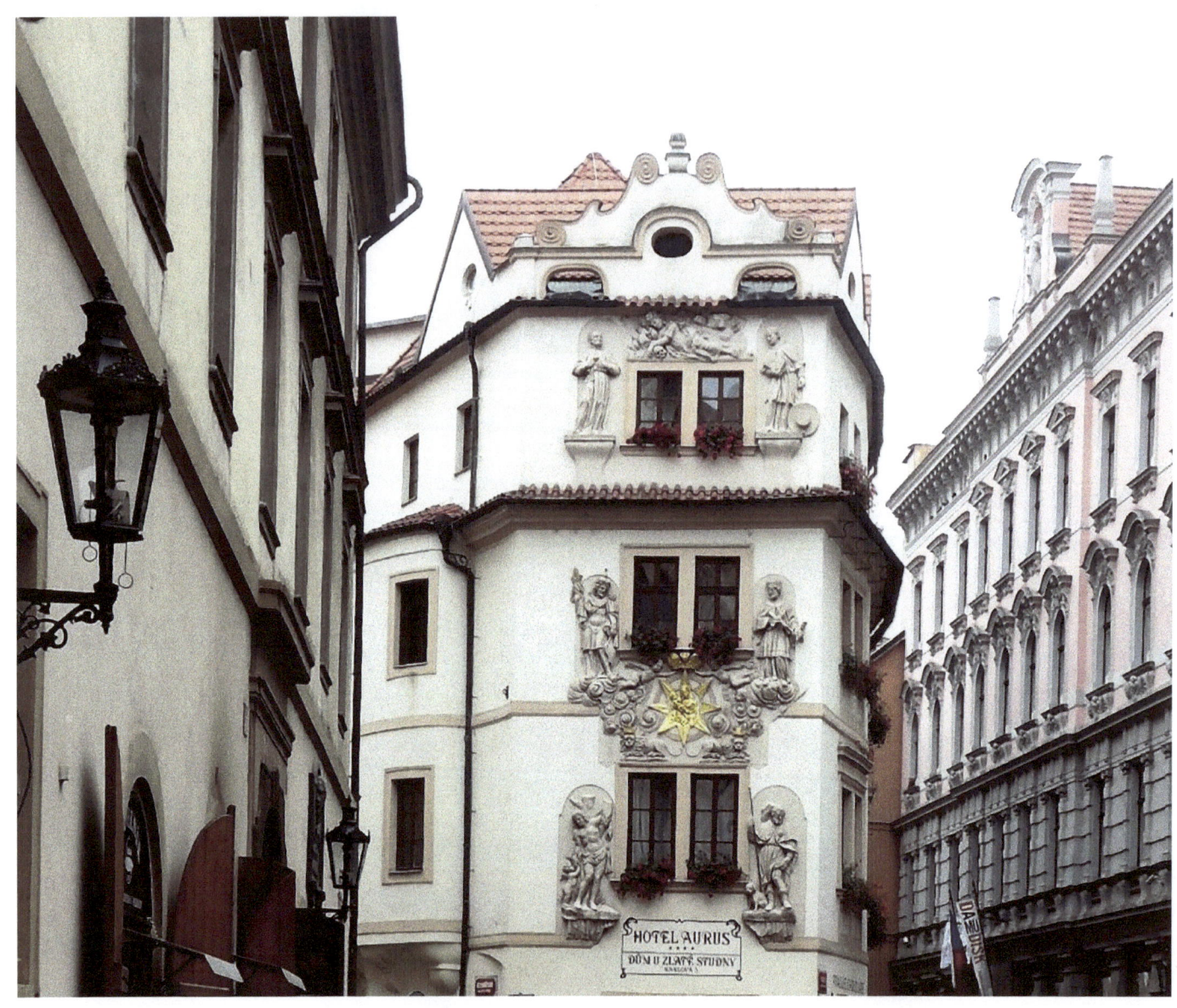

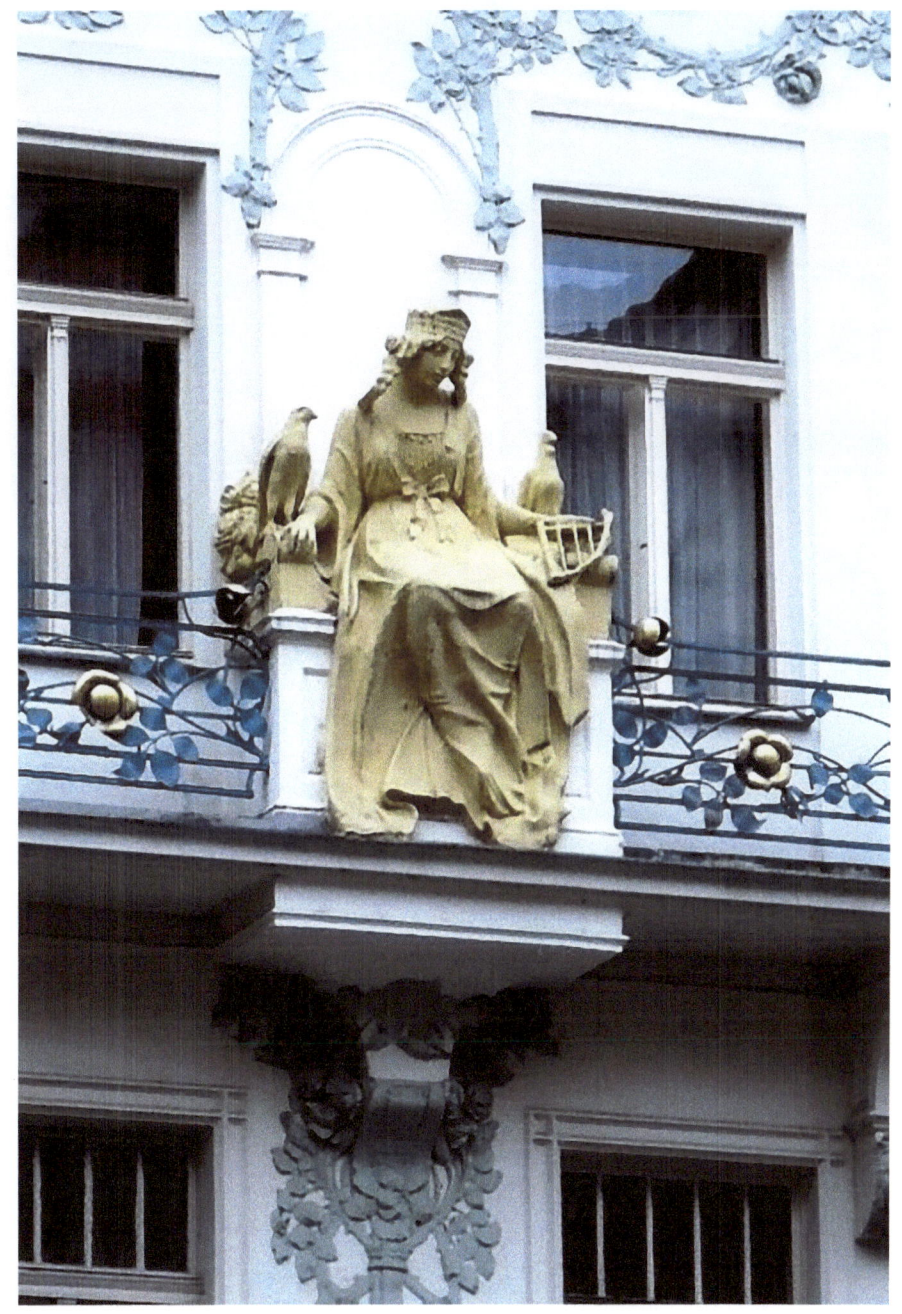

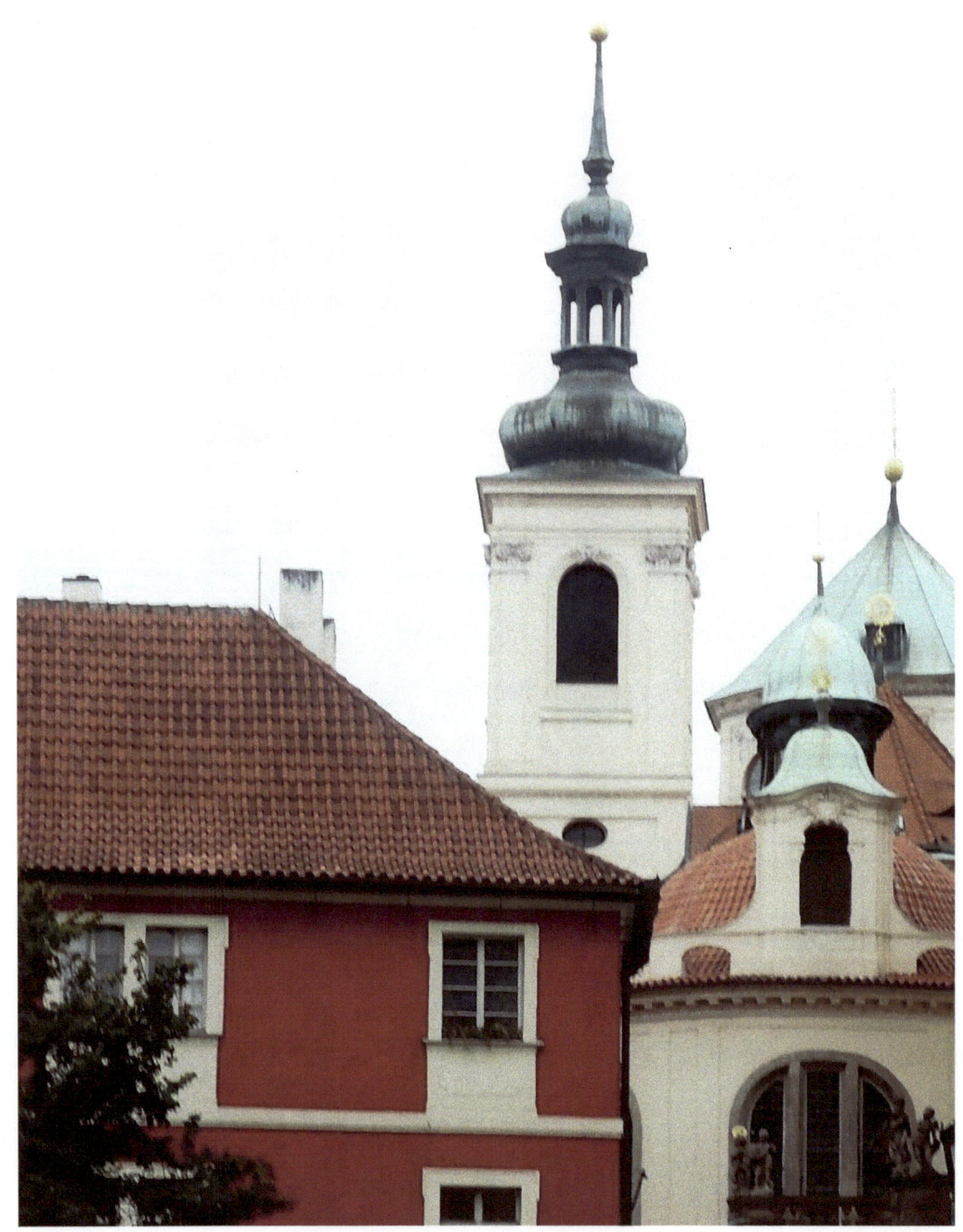

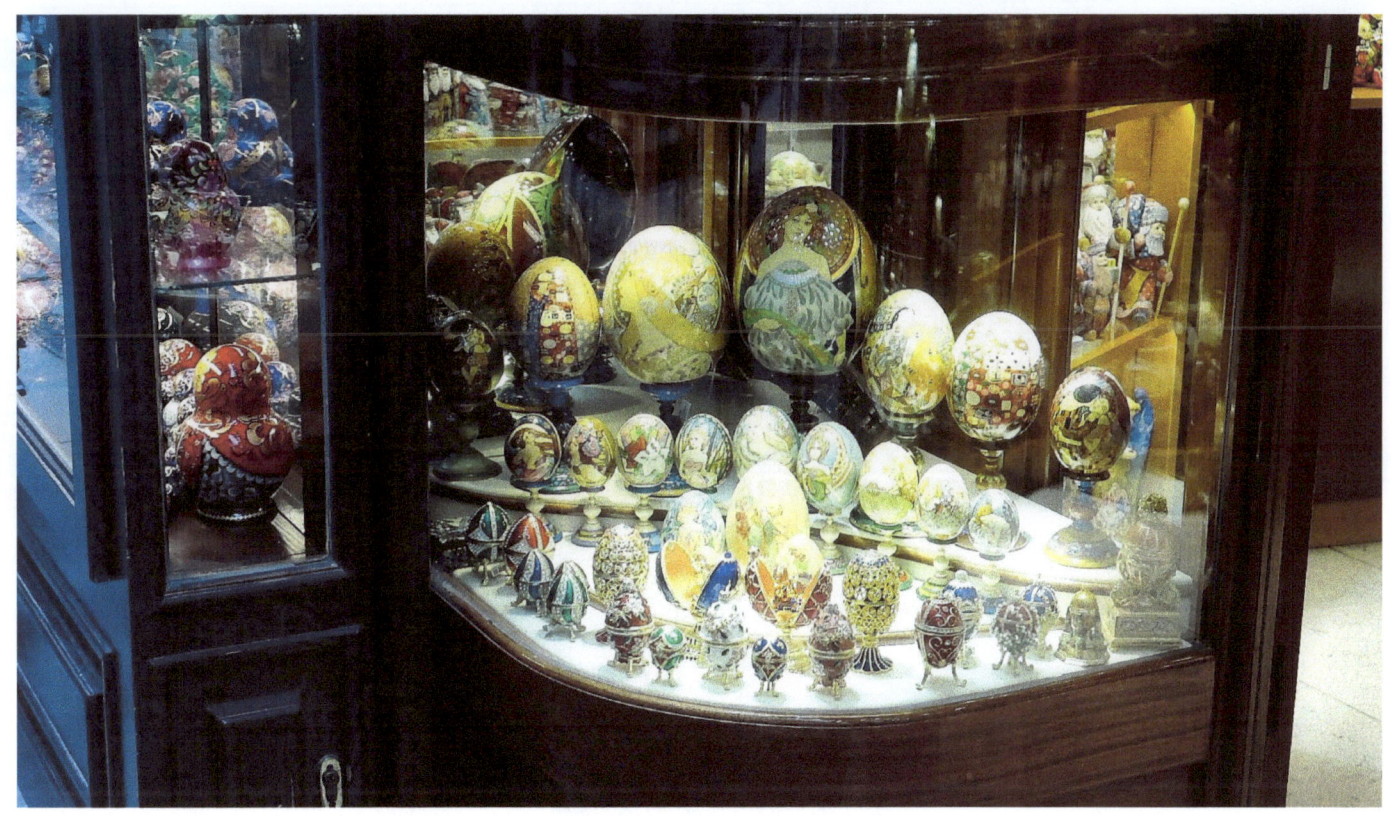

Koleno, *baked pork knee*. Also this typical Czech dish is based on meat, on the contrary it consists of a whole pig's leg marinated in dark beer mixed with aromatic herbs. The result is crunchy on the outside, tender and juicy on the inside. The cooking process, in fact, makes the meat so soft that it can separate from the bone on its own. Obviously the procedure is very long, about 45 minutes, which you can use by tasting some local beer. First cut the skin in the form of a grill right on the meat. Penetrate by rubbing garlic, mustard, salt, cumin and pepper. Then put the meat in the pan and let it cool for at least 2 hours in the fridge (better one day). After seasoning, add the pimento and bay leaves to the meat, sprinkle with the chopped onion, add twig of rosemary or juniper and pour the beer. Cover the pan with aluminum foil and roast in an oven at 200° for about 1.5 hours. Occasionally wet with water to wet the meat. Remove the foil and cook for half an hour to roast the meat until it is crispy. Remove the ready leg from the pan, drain the sauce and take out the spices. As needed, reduce or thicken with a thickener or bread that you have previously mixed with the blender. Serve with bread, horseradish, cucumber, or potato and spinach gnocchi.

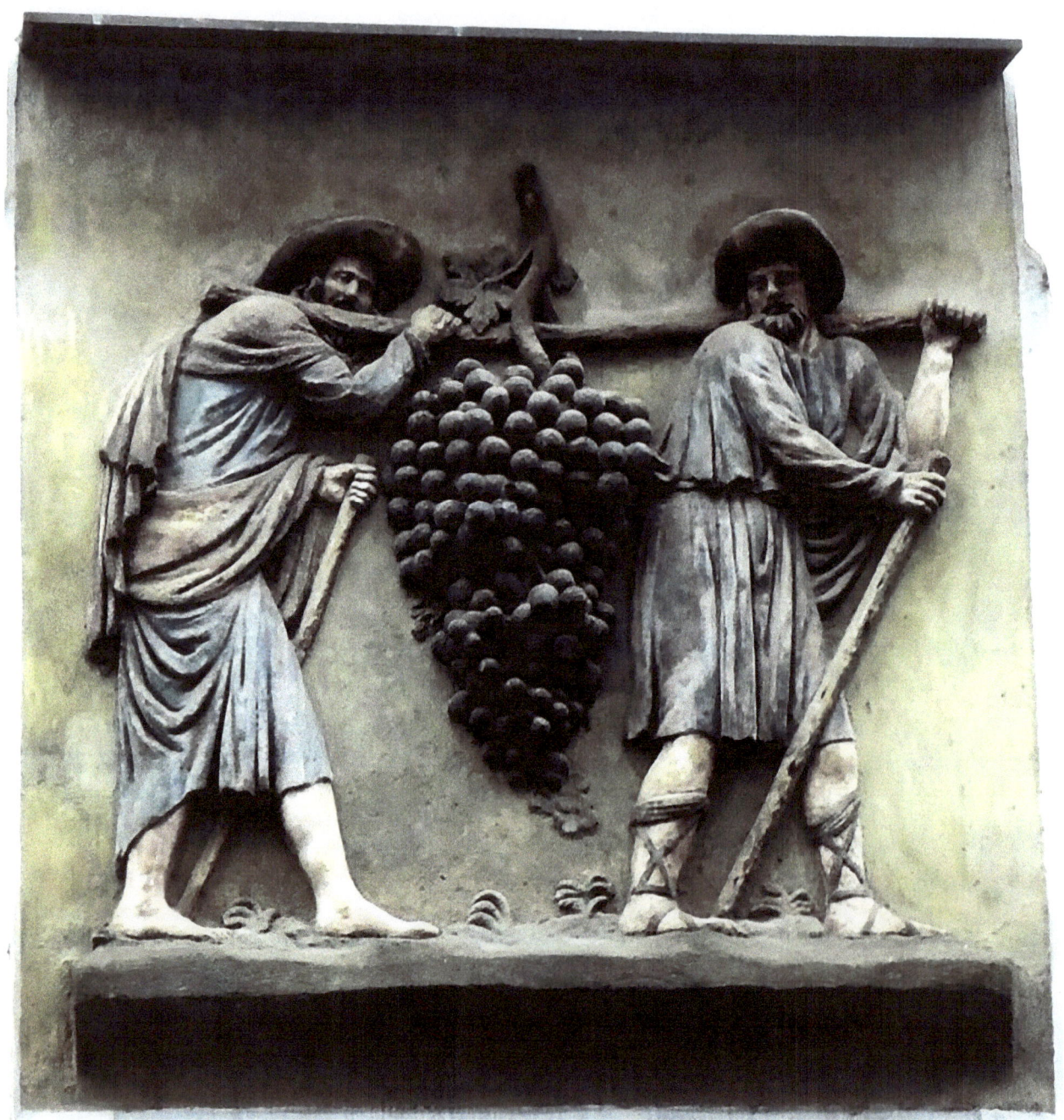

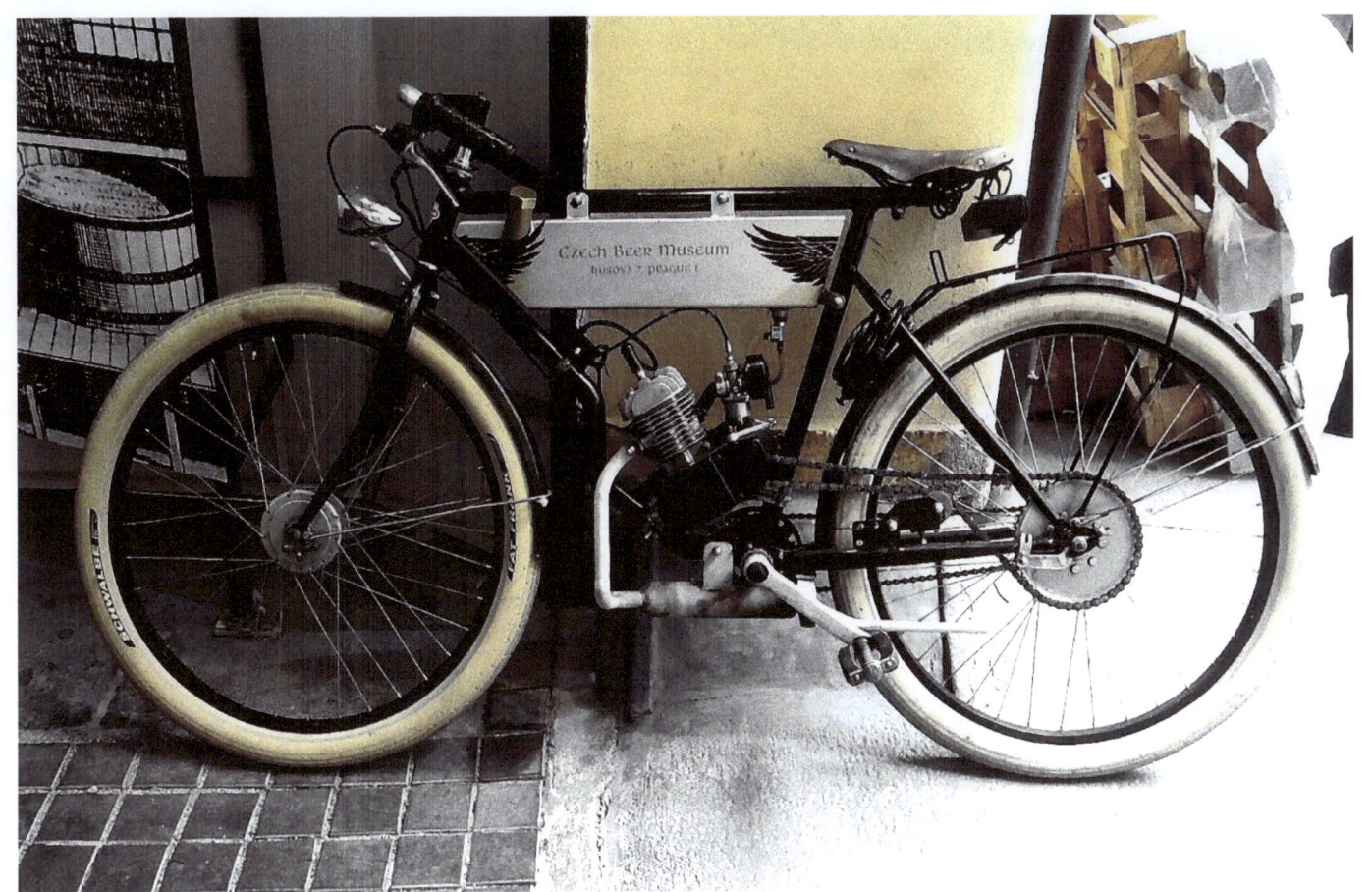

Pecena Kachna, *roast duck, usually accompanied by smoked bacon dumplings and red sauerkraut*. Carefully wash and dry a duck inside and out. Cut off the tips of the wings and excess oily skin around the neck and from the cavity. Pierce the duck with a fork, without piercing the meat. Liberate the outside and inside of the duck abundantly, rub with garlic and sprinkle with cumin. Place the duck breast in a pan with a lid. If the duck has just come out of the refrigerator, let it rest for about 2 hours to reach room temperature. Heat the oven to 180°. Pour a cup of water at the bottom of the pan. Roast the duck an hour and cream off excess fat. Salt the duck breast and continue to roast uncovered for another hour until the skin is golden. Remove from the oven and let stand 10 minutes before serving.

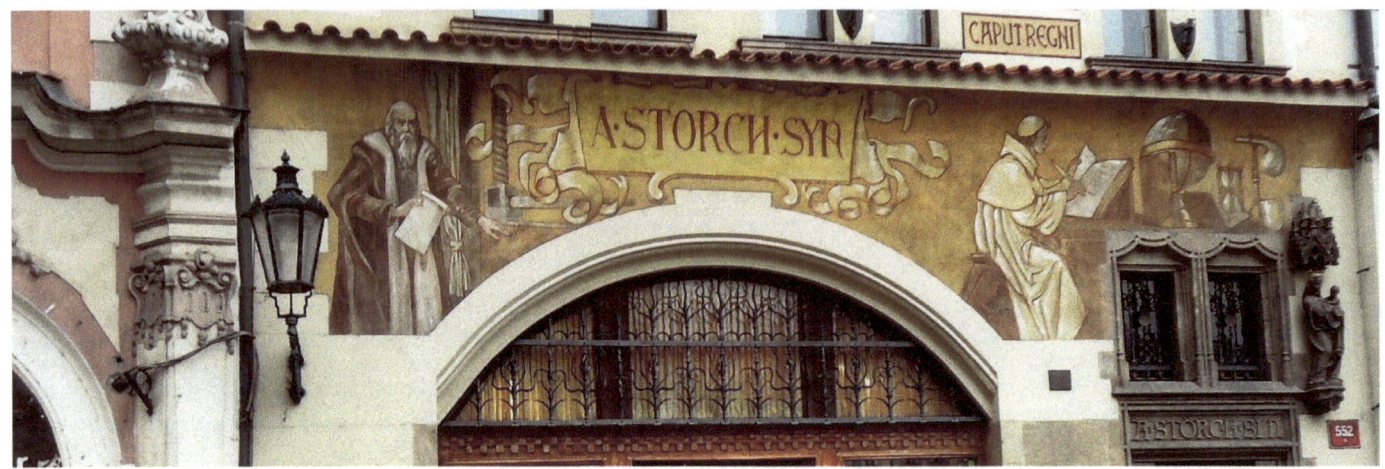

Pivni gulash, *beer goulash*. Cut a kilo of onions into very thin slices and fry them in a pan with a little oil. Cut almost the same weight of beef into cubes of two centimeters, flour them and, after adding paprika, brown them in a non-stick pan (which will have to go into the oven) and blend with a little beer. Add the onions, the remaining 33 cl. of Czech beer, water, thyme, a tube of concentrated tomato, salt and pepper. Once the water is warm, move the covered pan into the preheated 110° oven. Leave an hour in the oven. The goulash is the typical dish that improves if heated.

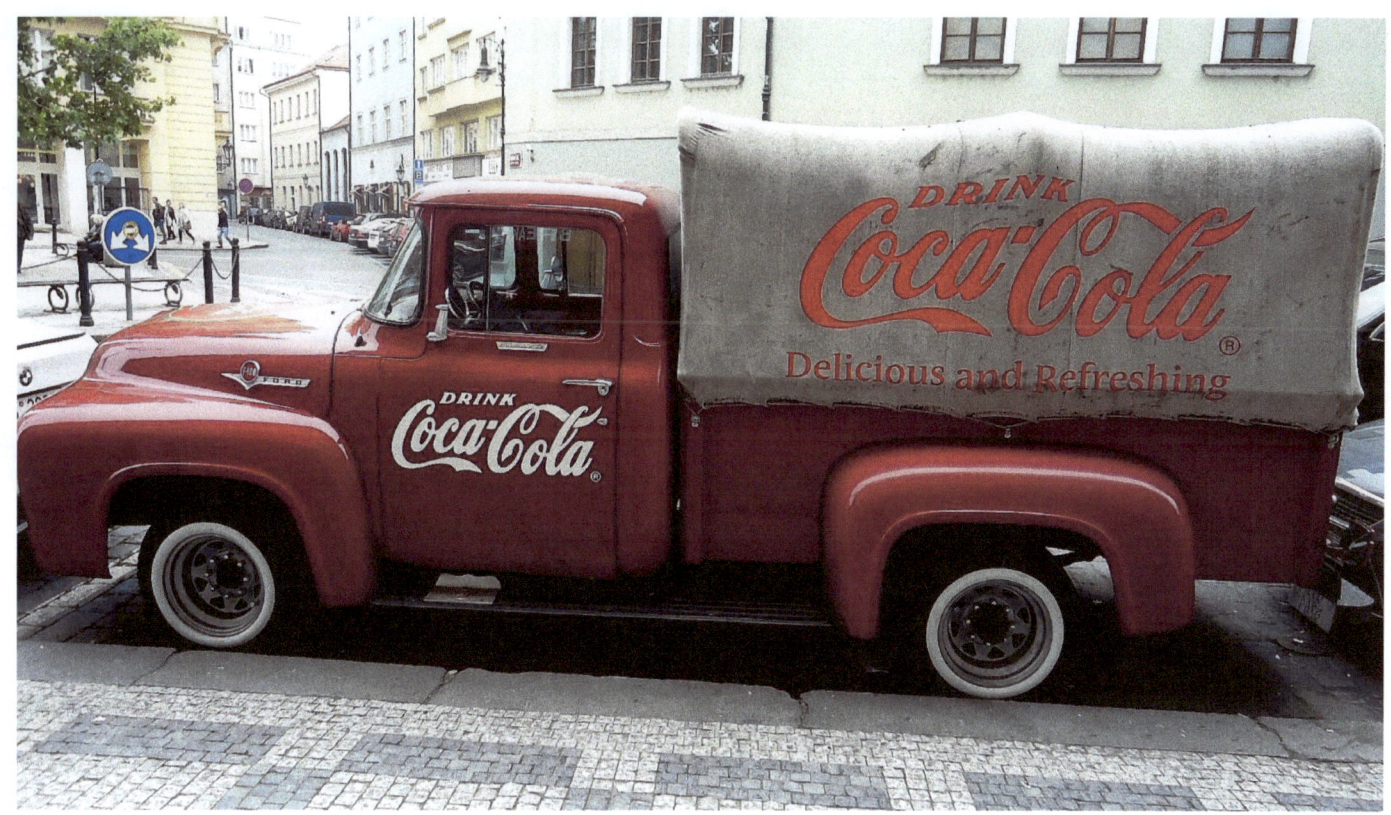

Svíčková na smetaně, *roast beef fillet in casserole, served with cream and carrot sauce and garnished with whipped cream and blueberries*. Clean a beef sirloin, remove the membrane and fill with bacon. Then add salt and pepper. Clean an onion, cut it into small pieces and grate the clean vegetables. Put the meat in the pan, add two carrots, celery, parsley, bay leaves, thyme, pour the lemon juice and the melted butter. Cover and season in the fridge for a day.

The next day moisten with a little water and cook stewed in the oven until it is tender. Then take the meat out to let it rest. Remove the spices from the sauce, especially the bay leaf and slowly cook the sauce in the pan. Add the mustard, sprinkle with 2 tablespoons of flour and sauté a little in the pan. Pour the cream and cook stirring occasionally. If the sauce is too thick, dilute it with milk. Finally drain it and sift the soft vegetables into the sauce. Season with salt, add lemon juice or sweeten. To enhance the taste, you can add a little caramel. Make portions of the meat, put them in the sauce and heat. Serve with the bread dumplings decorated with a slice of lemon and the cranberry mixture.

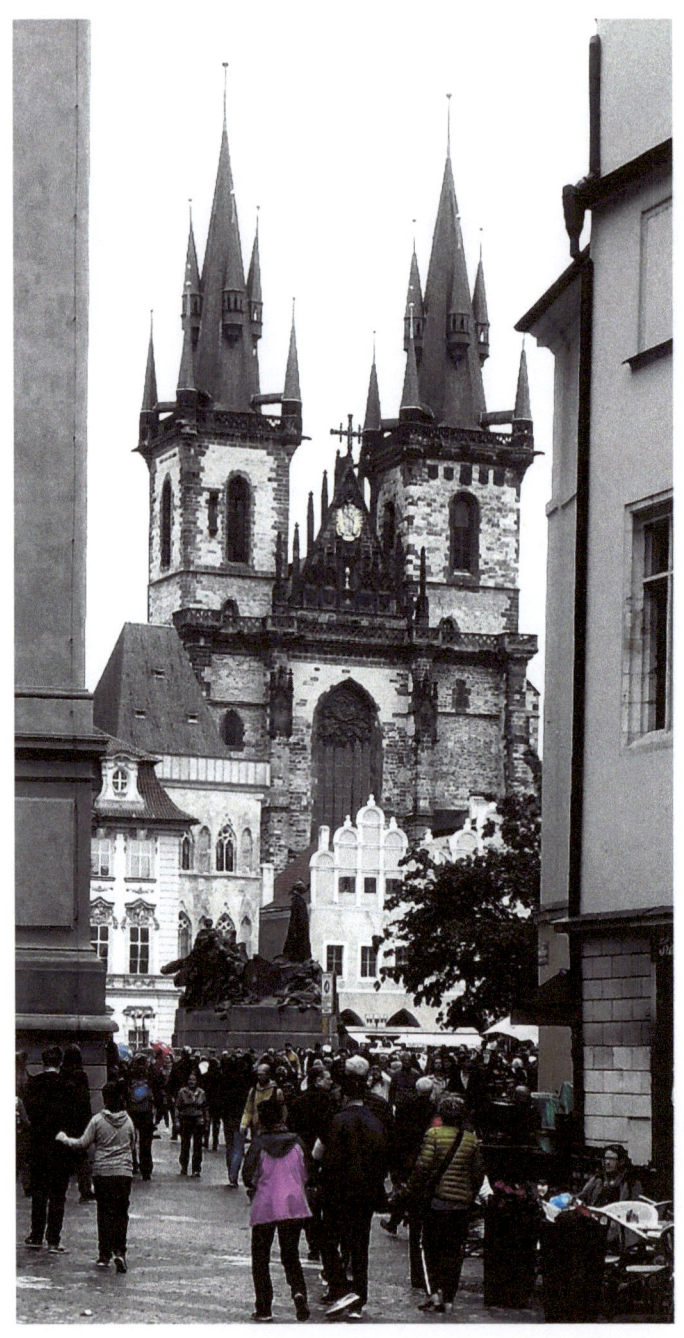

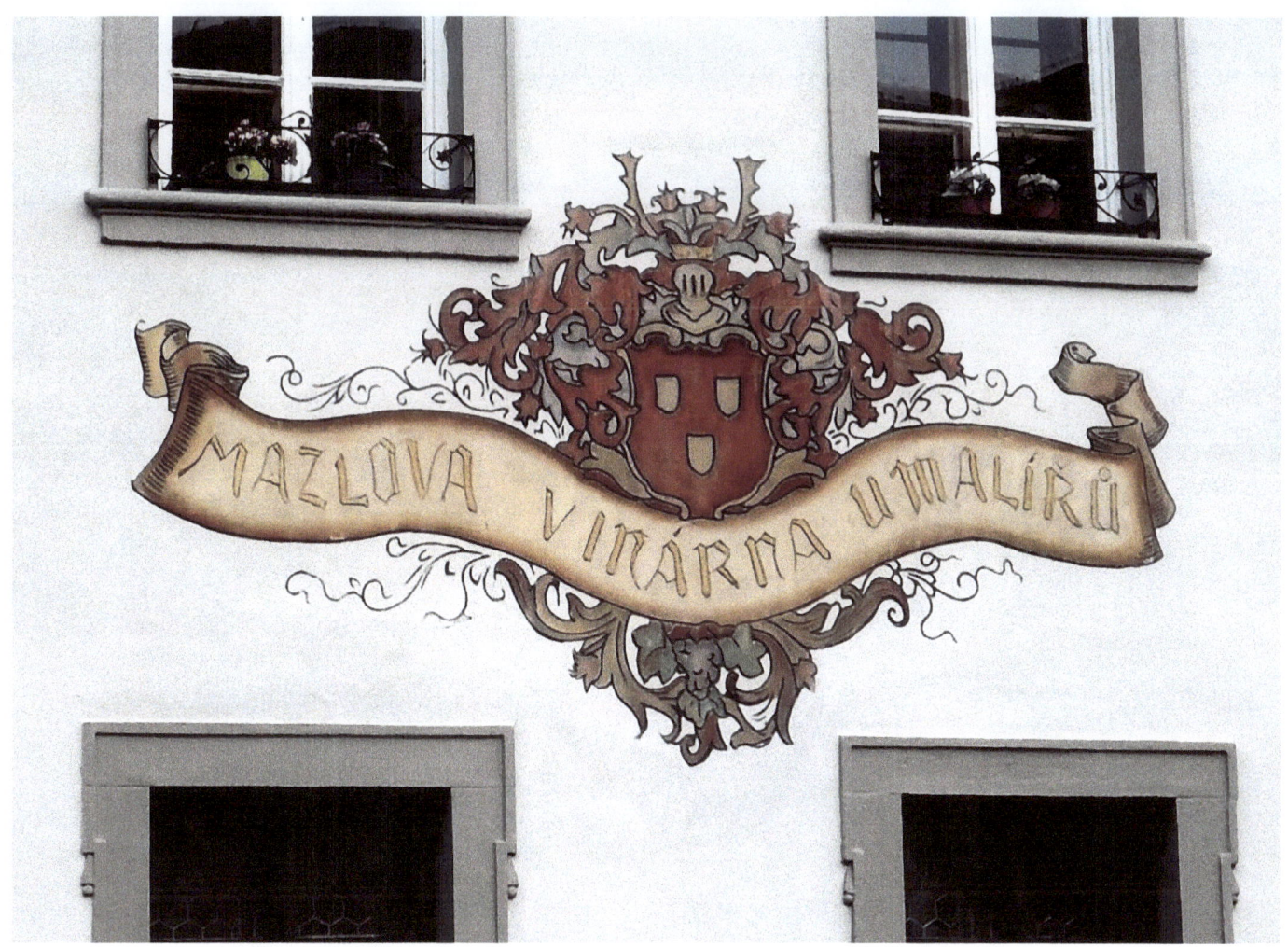

Smažený Sýr, *fried cheese*. Prepare a batter with flour, beaten egg and milk and mix it until it becomes smooth and thick, but not too dry. Adjust with the quantities and if necessary add more flour or milk. Then dip a slice of cheese first in the batter then in the breadcrumbs placed in a shallow dish. Repeat the procedure again so that the cheese does not come out during frying. Fry the smažený sýr in abundant oil and drain them when they are golden brown on both sides. Let them dry briefly on absorbent paper and serve them still warm when the cheese is still stringy with the salad and tartar sauce.

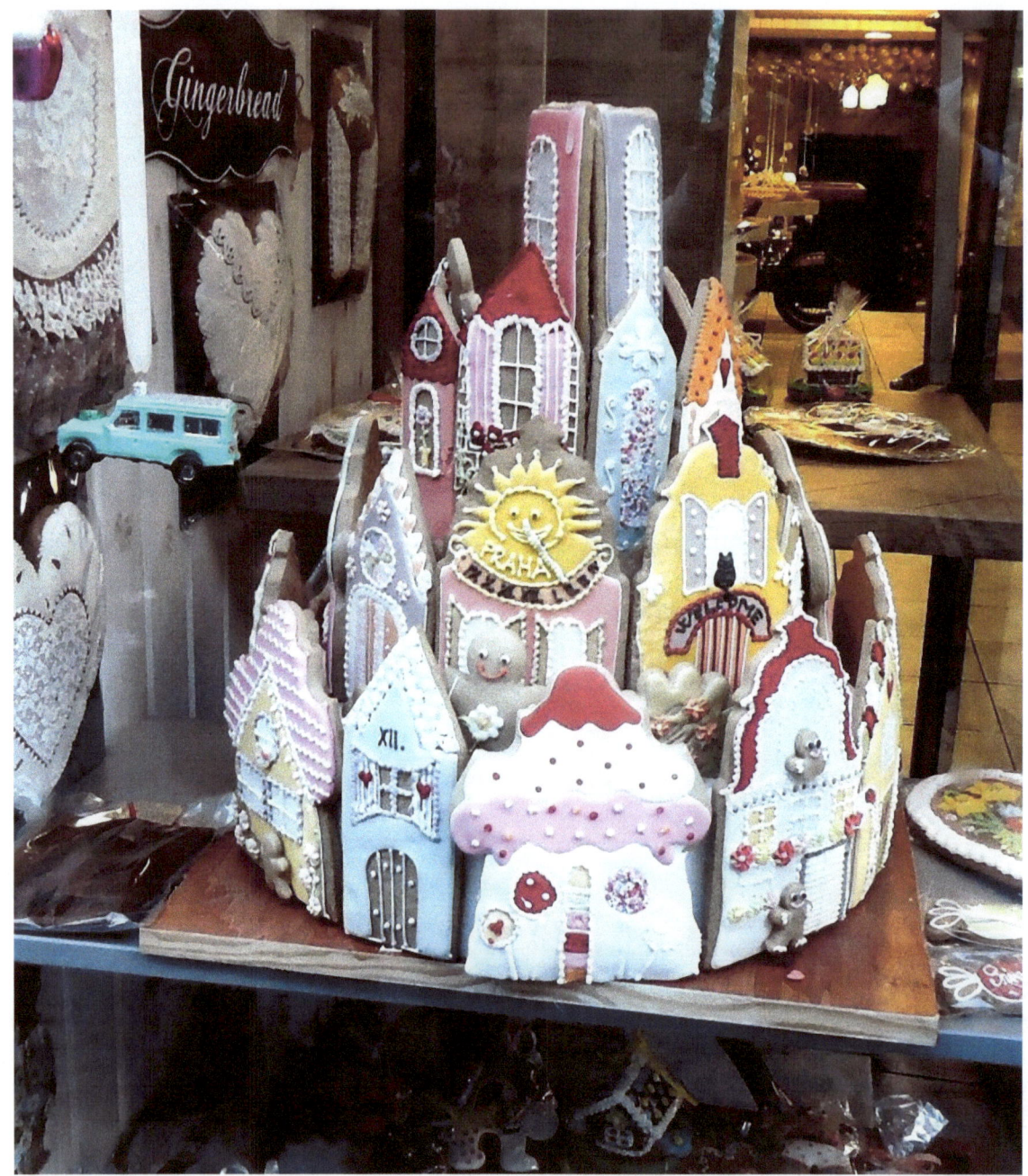

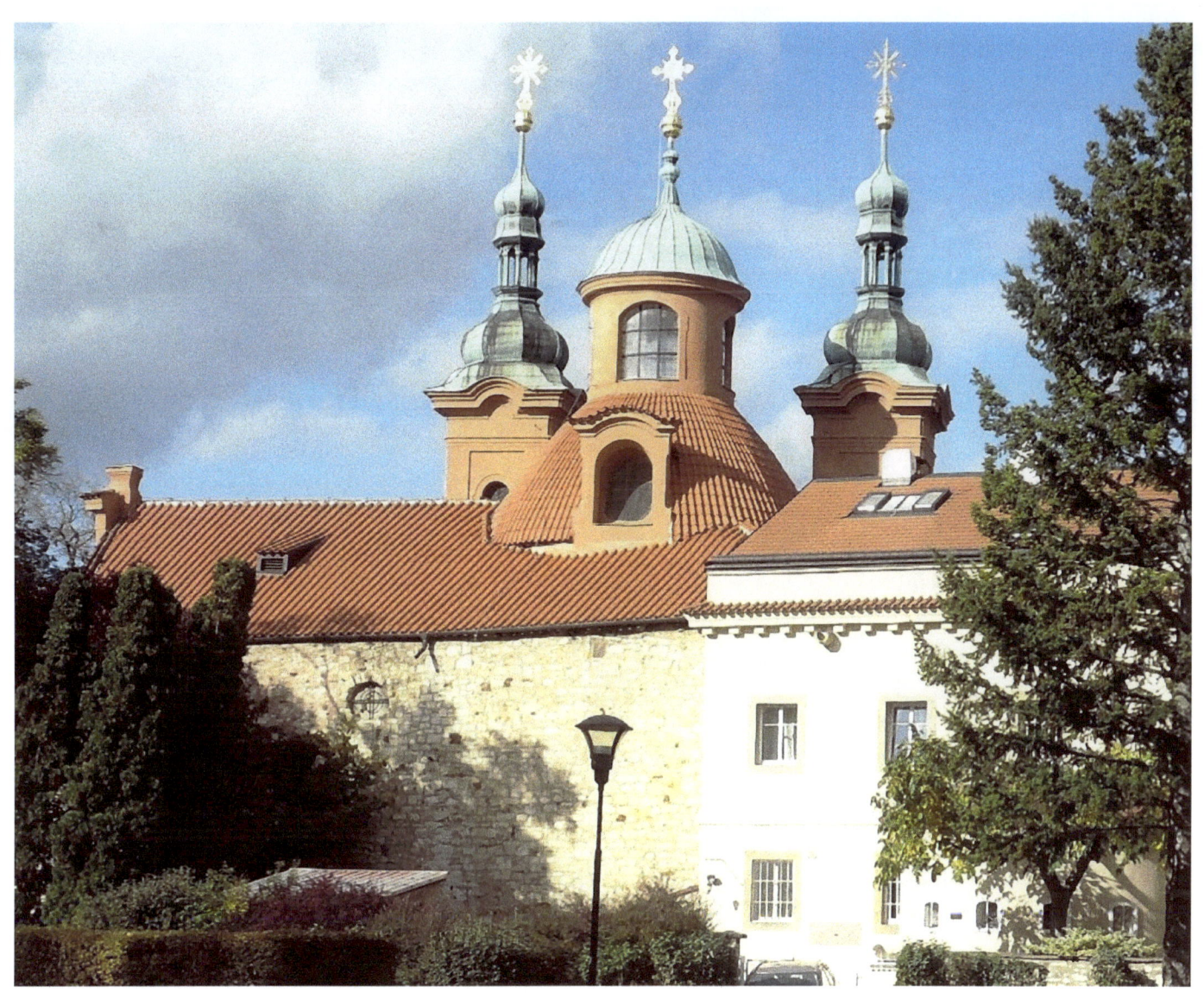

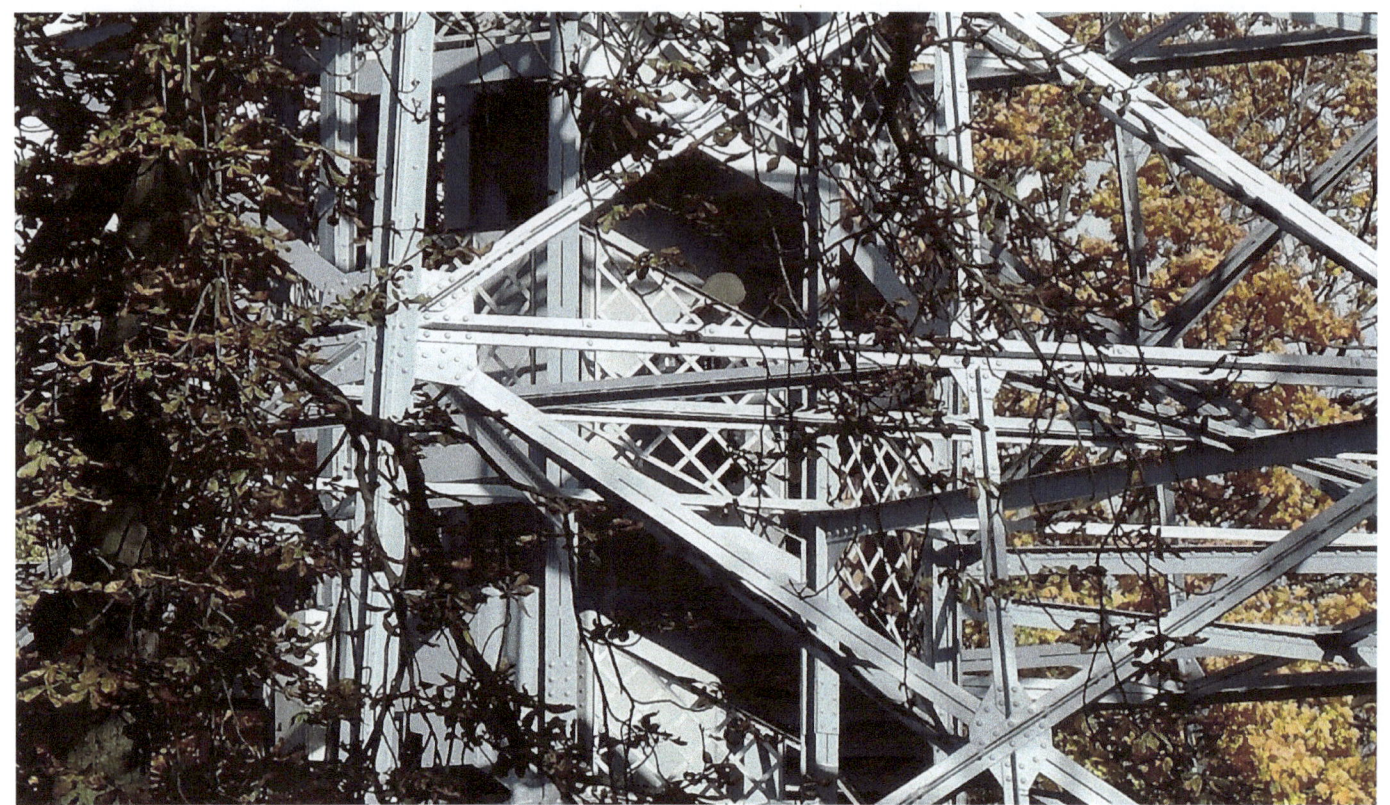

Uzené, *smoked pork*. Peel the cooked potatoes with the peel and cut them into slices. Also cut the smoked pork neck through the thicker sliced fiber. Preheat the oven to 200° C. Place the pan with slices of bacon, half a portion of potatoes, season with salt and pepper and distribute the sliced onion and a little sauerkraut on the potatoes. Sprinkle with juniper berries, bay leaves, cloves and distribute the minced smoked meat, then the remaining sauerkraut and potatoes. Salt on the surface, pour over the cream with the mixed peppers and place in a preheated oven. Cook for 30-40 minutes until the potatoes turn golden and the sauerkraut soften. Let it rest a little before serving.

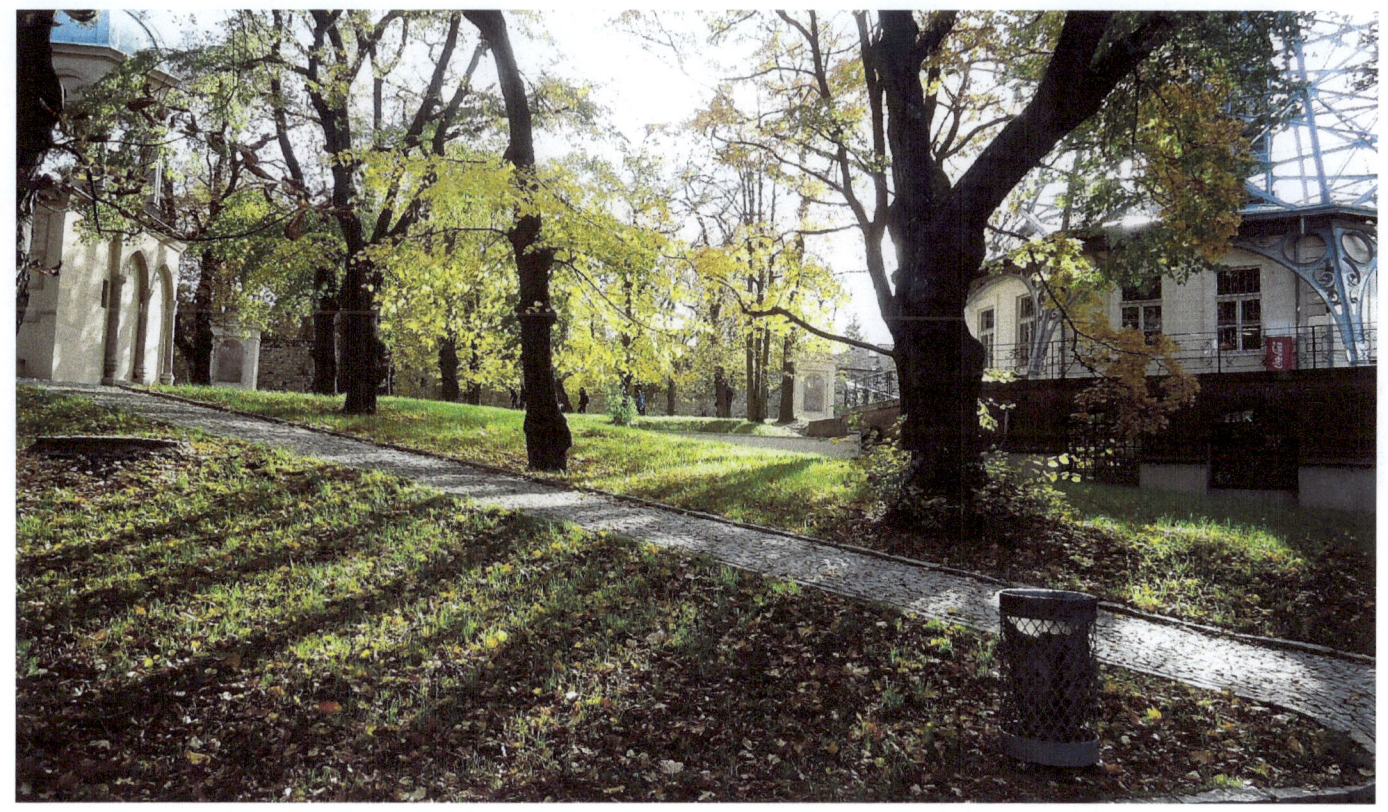

Vepřoknedlozelo, *pork with sauerkraut and dumplings*. **Gnocchi**: cut the crusts from the white bread and cut the bread into cubes. Add two beaten eggs, milk and a pinch of salt. Mix everything until a solid mass is formed. Let the mass rest for half an hour. Mix the dough again and make some balls. Let the balls rest for half an hour and then fry them in hot oil until golden brown.
Meat: during the time when the meatball dough has to rest you can start preparing the meat. Season the pork chops with salt, cumin and a little garlic. Cook them until they are light brown, then add the water and a nut. Boil over low heat for an hour or until cooked.
Sauerkraut: while cooking the meat you can prepare sauerkraut. Cut the onions into strips and fry them until they are light brown. Cook the sauerkraut in water and then add salt, cumin and onions. Finally add white wine vinegar and sugar.

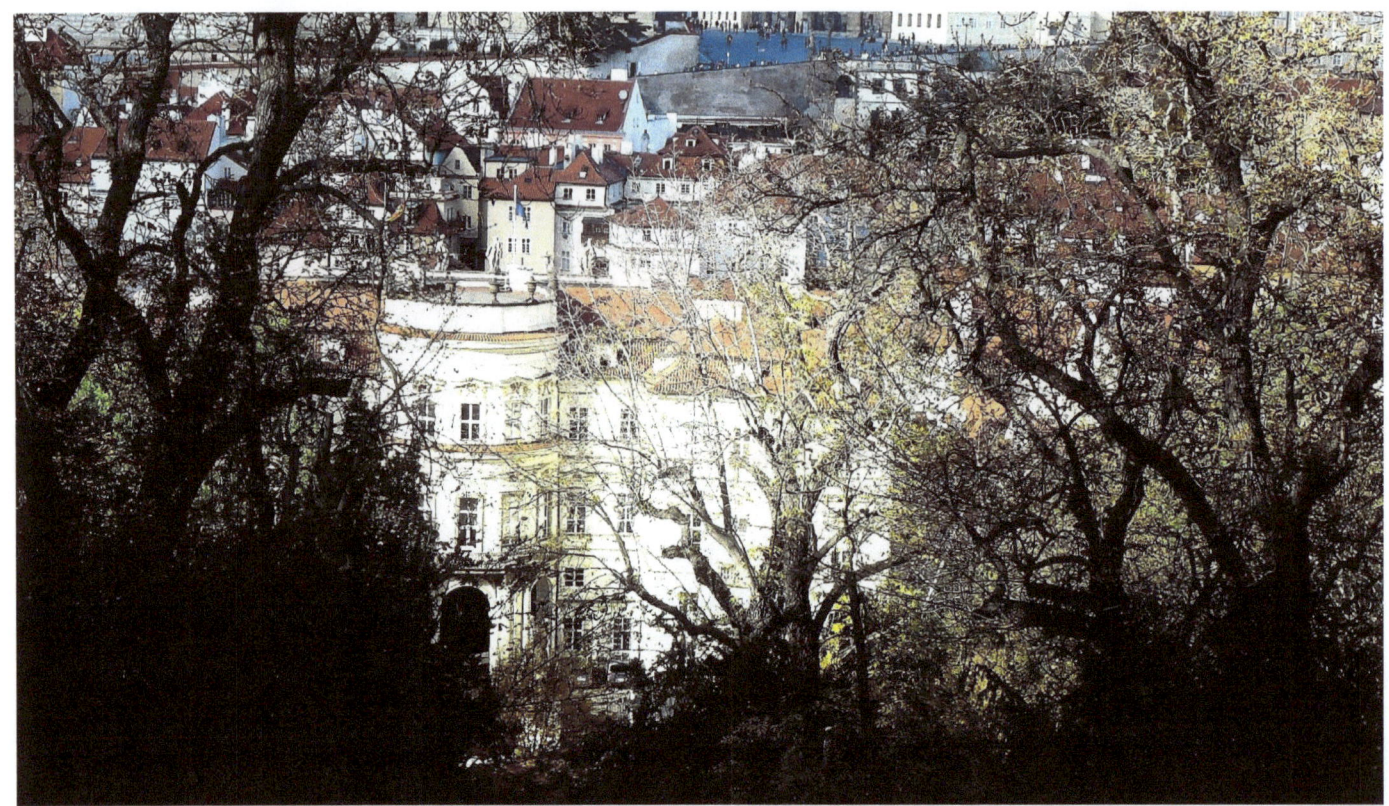

Bramborové knedlíky, *potato dumplings*. Cook the potatoes with the peel. The next day peel them and grate them on a coarse grater. Add coarse semolina flour and regular flour, salt and eggs. Mix everything with your hands and work hard. When the mixture has been worked correctly roll it into two or three large dumplings. Dip the gnocchi in boiling salted water and cook for 10-12 minutes, 6 minutes on one side and then turn them. After removing the dumplings from the water, pierce them with a stick to prevent them from sticking and slice them with the wire. Grandma's potato gnocchi serve as an excellent side dish for meat, spinach or sauerkraut.

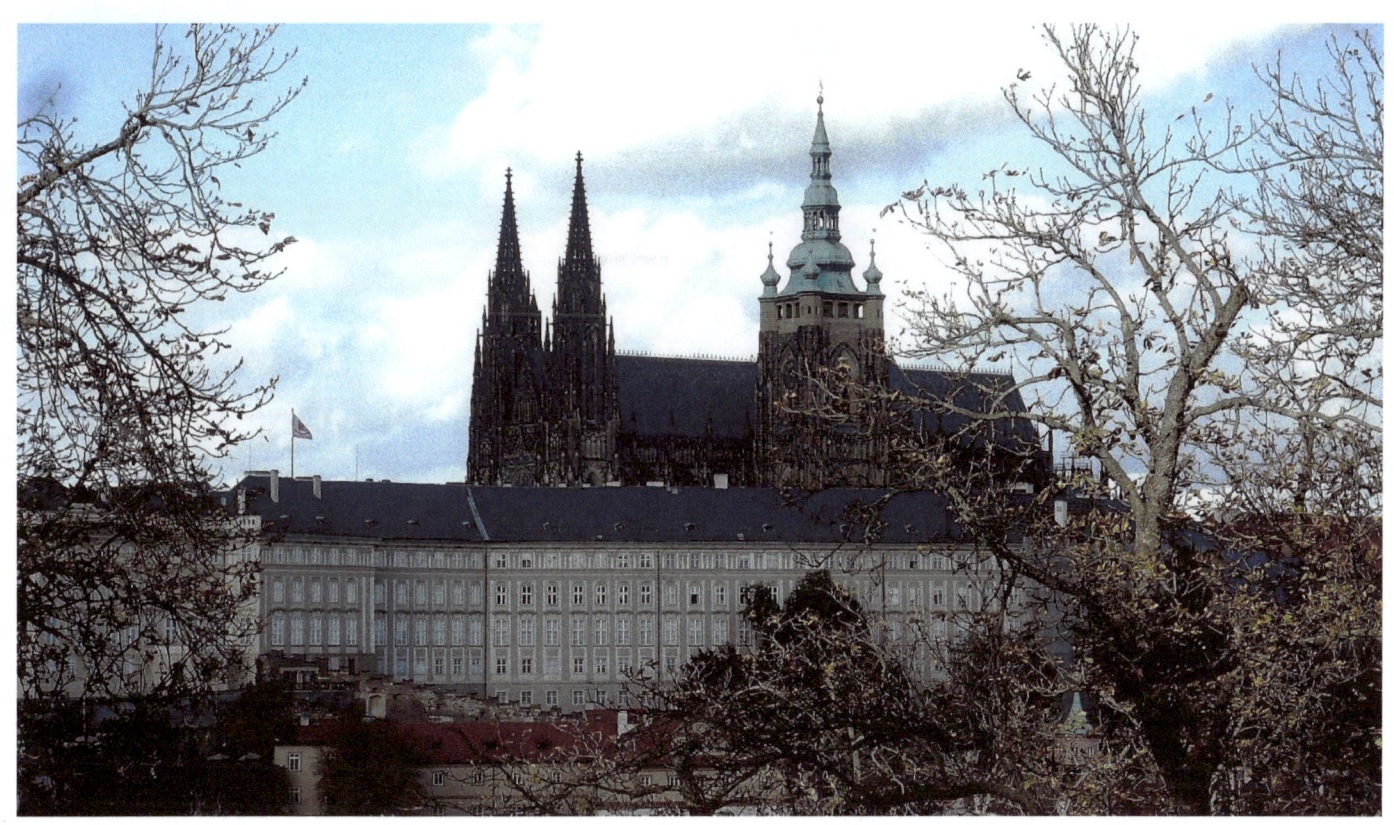

Bramborový salát, *Christmas potato salad*. The day before you cook the potatoes with the peel, the root vegetables (celery and carrots) and the boiled eggs. The root vegetables are cleaned and cooked in a brine containing a bay leaf, allspice, pepper, salt, sugar and a tablespoon of vinegar. Let the vegetables cool. Peel the potatoes and squeeze or cut them into cubes. Also cut the boiled vegetables, cucumbers and onions into small pieces. Put everything on the potatoes and add a can of peas. Mix mayonnaise carefully (possibly with a little white yogurt), mustard, oil, salt and ground pepper. Finally add the chopped boiled eggs and season with the brine in which you cook the vegetables. Mix the classic Christmas potato salad again and let it cool. The classic Christmas potato salad must be prepared early in the morning so that it fits well in the evening.

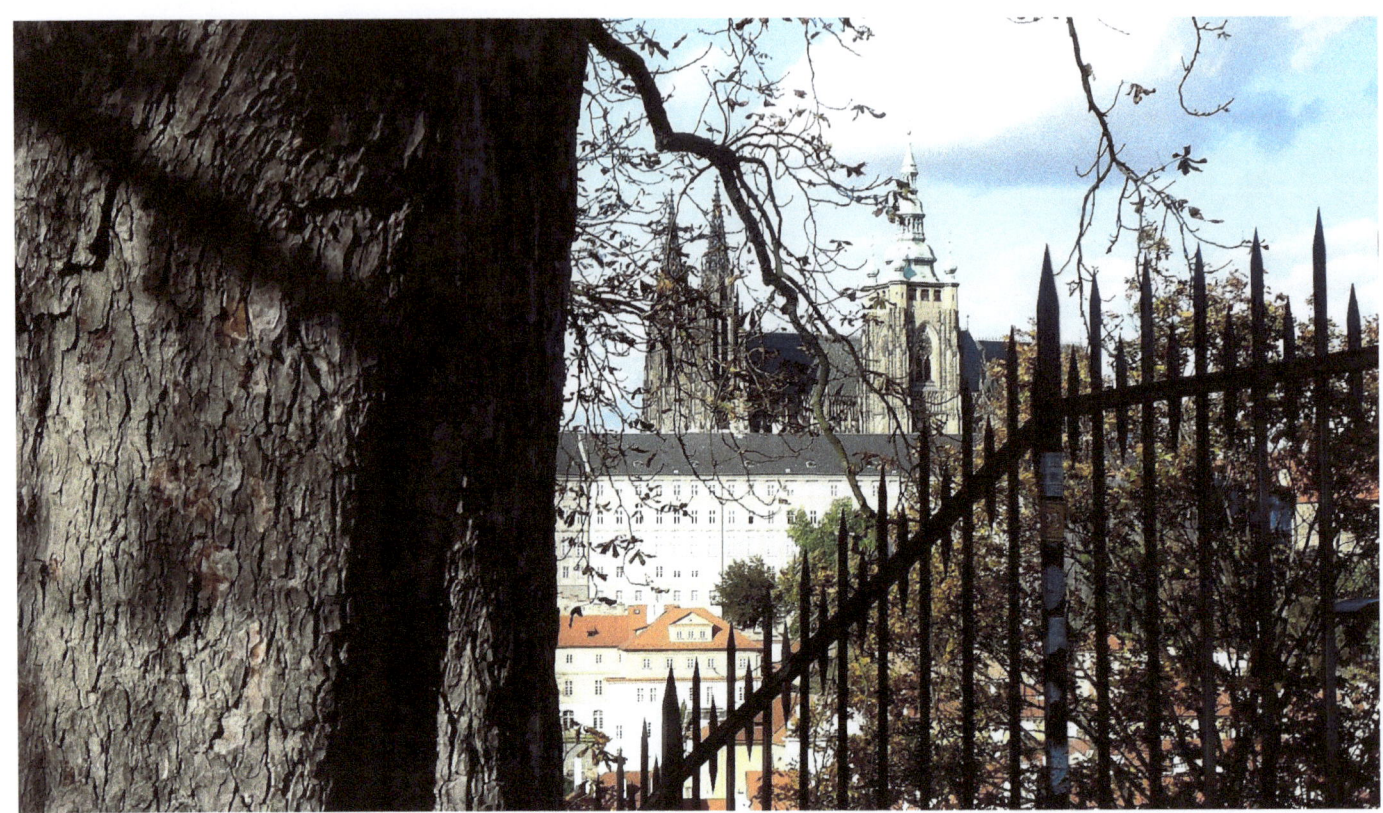

Zelí, *bread dumplings or potatoes with sauerkraut*. Decant the cabbage, let it drain and slice it. Pour it into water, add cumin and cook over a low heat until it is semi-soft. In hot oil, fry the diced onion and add it to the cabbage. Peel and grate the potato on a fine grater, add a tablespoon of flour and stir. Thicken the cabbage with this mixture and cook over a low heat for a while. Finally add the vinegar, sugar and salt to taste.

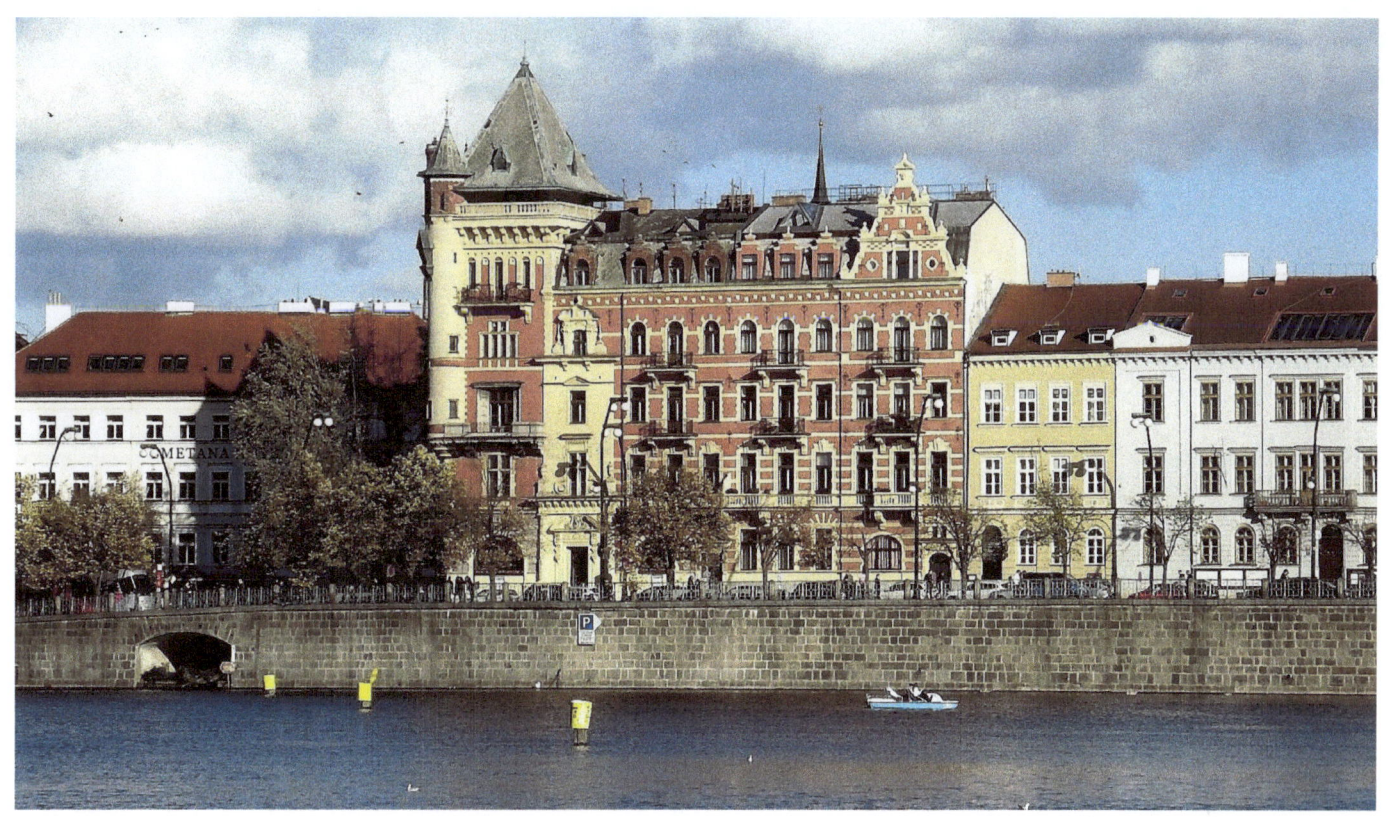

Borůvkové knedlíky, *blueberry dumplings*. Put large flour, salt and sugar in a bowl and stir. Make a hollow in the mixture and crush the yeast. Sprinkle with sugar, add the milk and let the sourdough rise. Then add more milk, the egg and knead. Let rise in a warm place for about 30 minutes. Divide the leavened dough into 6 pieces, roll them each on a pie and fill them with blueberries, shape them into a dumpling and let them rise for 15 minutes. Then place the gnocchi in boiling salted water (cook them for 3-5 minutes on one side and 3 minutes on the other side) or steam them, it takes about 15 minutes. After cooking, tear the gnocchi lightly or pierce them with a fork to prevent the steam from escaping and sticking. Serve the gnocchi seasoned with butter, ricotta or sweetened sour cream.

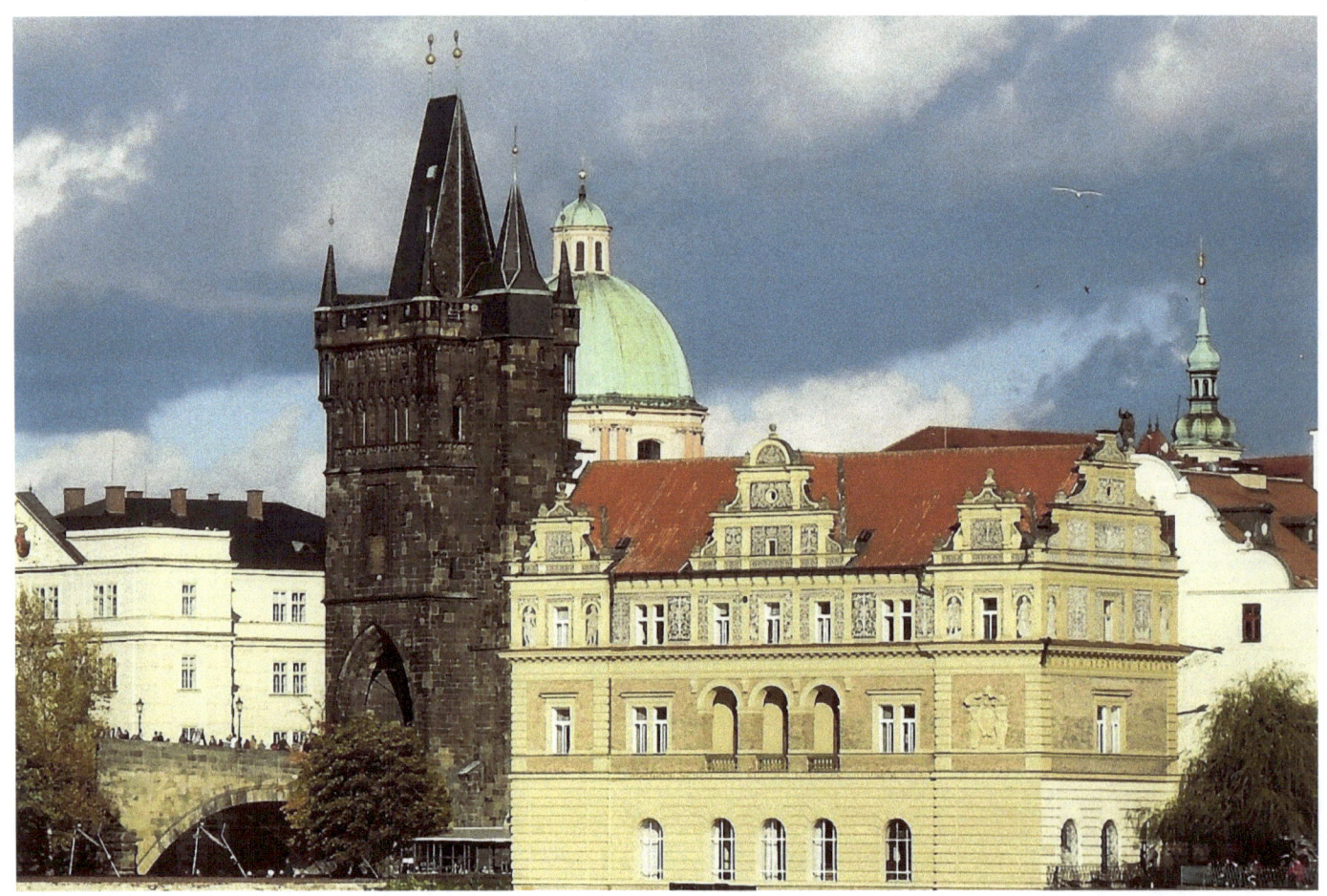

Jablečný závin, *apple strudel*. Sprinkle the puff pastry with a layer of breadcrumbs (so that the apple juice does not spill out). Grate the apples and mix them with raisins and walnuts. Put the apple mixture on the dough with breadcrumbs. Sprinkle with cinnamon and sugar. Roll the dough to form a strudel and brush it with the egg. Cook for about 20 minutes in a preheated oven (about 200° C).

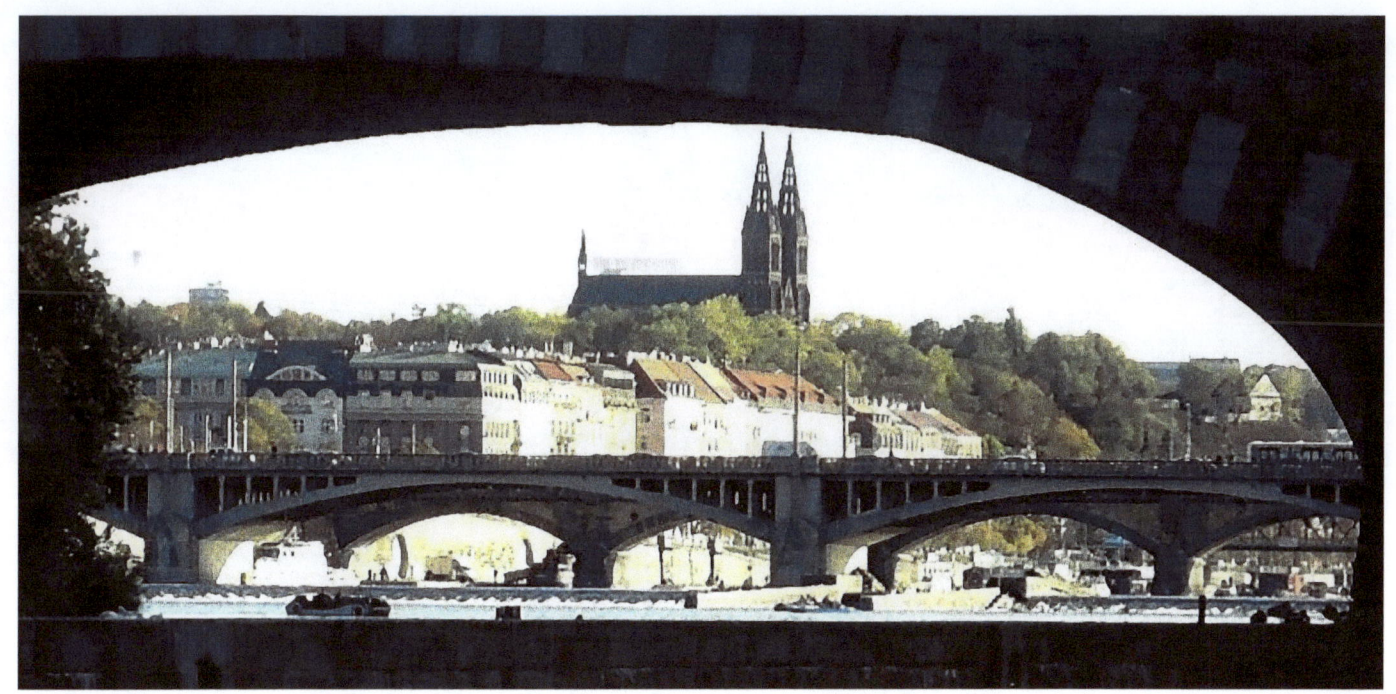

Palačinky, *crepes stuffed with jam or chocolate*. Prepare the dough with flour, eggs, milk and salt. Mix everything well with a mixer until a liquid, lump-free mass is obtained. Fry the crepes one at a time on both sides in a special pancake pan on a knob of butter. To turn them, toss the pancakes in the air using the pan. Sprinkle with jam or chocolate, then roll them up or fold them in four and decorate with icing sugar, whipped cream, fruit, etc.

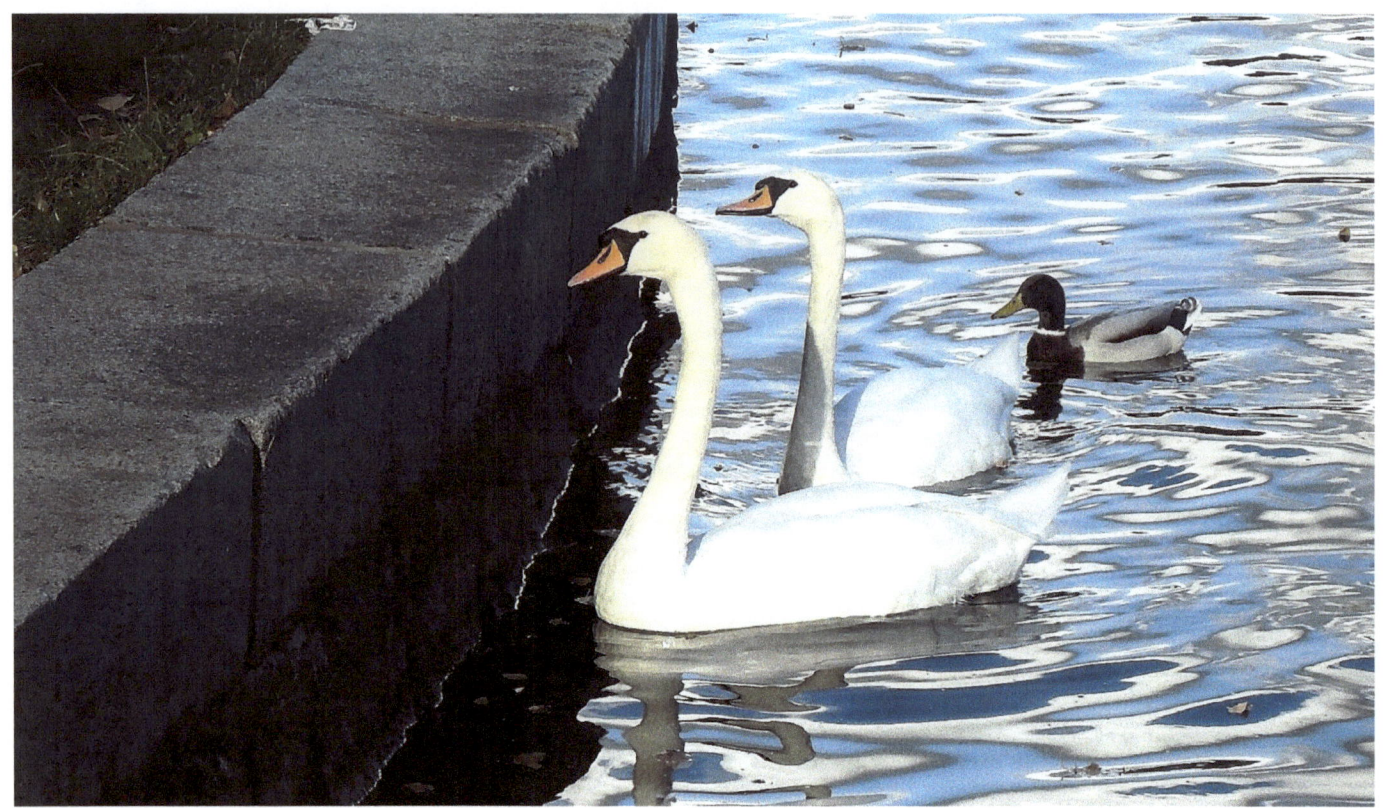

Trdelnik, *a typical Prague dessert*. Break the yeast into a bowl, add 3 teaspoons of sugar and dissolve it in a little warm milk. Let it sit for 5 minutes. Pour the flour and sugar into a bowl and begin to knead with the milk, after which add the egg, lightly beaten, the grated lemon rind and finally the chopped butter. Knead the dough well and then let it rise in a bowl for at least an hour and a half. Meanwhile prepare the coating for the Trdlo: mix the brown sugar and the powdered cinnamon on a flat plate. If you want, add chopped almonds or chocolate chips. When the dough has risen roll it out and cut eight strips of dough about a meter long and half a centimeter thick. At this point you will have to use a support to give your Trdelnik the classic cylindrical shape. You can buy rollers for Bohemian Sleeve or you can create an ad hoc roll. For this purpose I recommend using a steel rolling pin, then placing it on a baking sheet so that only the ends rest on the edge of the pan itself.

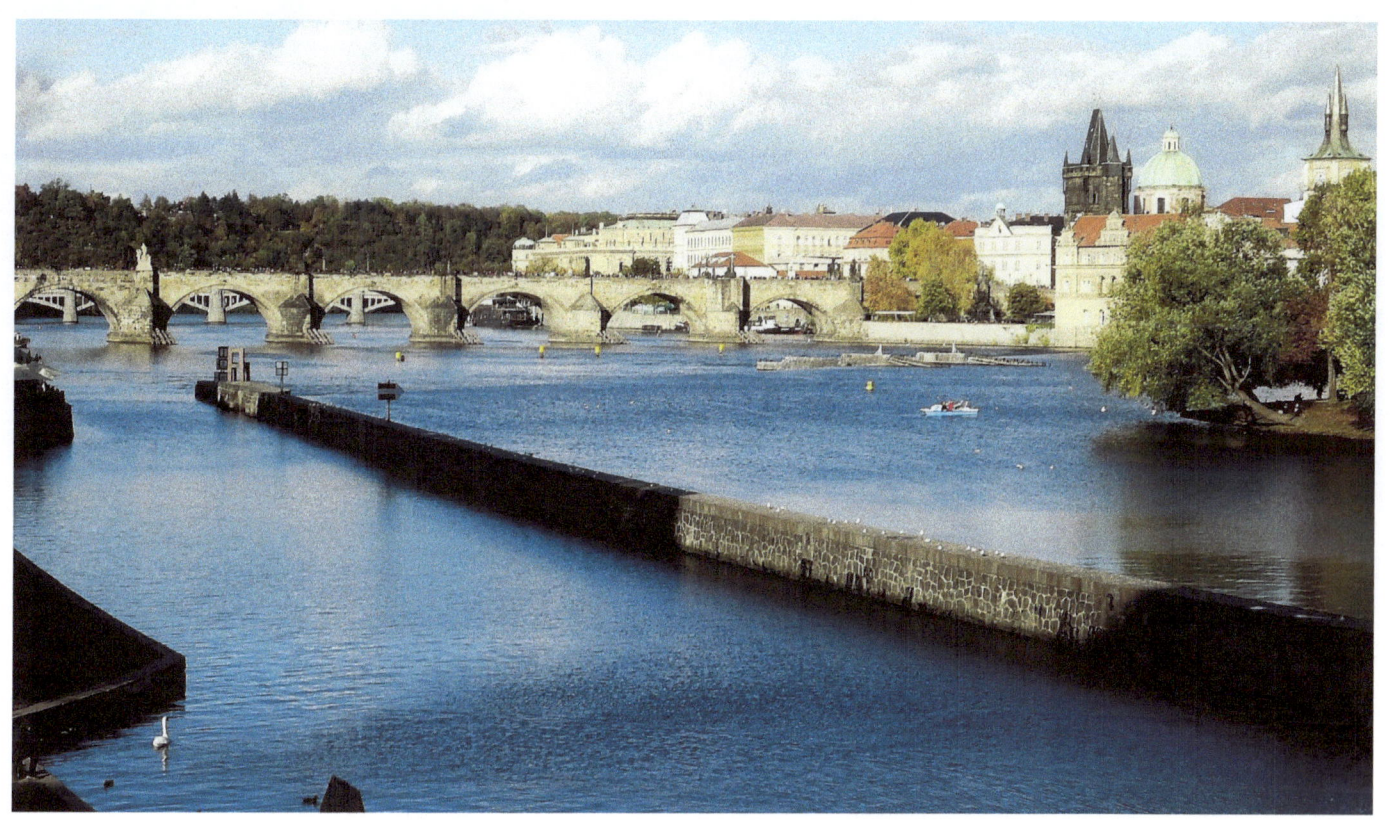

Once you have identified the support best suited to your needs, roll each strip of dough around the roll, being careful not to leave any space between turns. Brush each sleeve with egg white and bake for about 12-15 minutes in a preheated oven at 180° C (cooking time may vary from oven to oven). Once the pasta is cooked and the golden surface, take out the Trdlo, brush them with melted butter and pass them in the mix of brown sugar and cinnamon that you had prepared before. Now all you have to do is fill them with cream, chocolate or more.

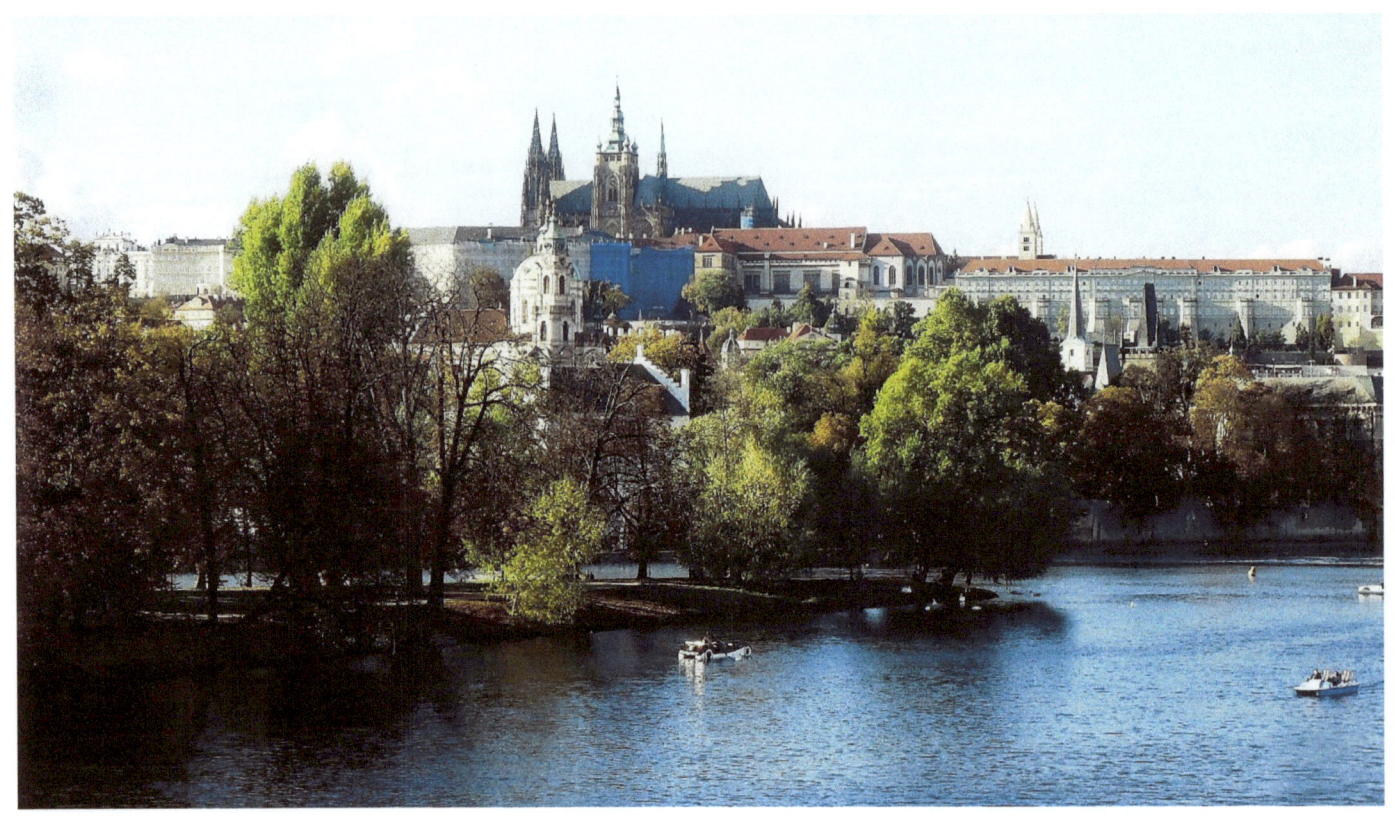

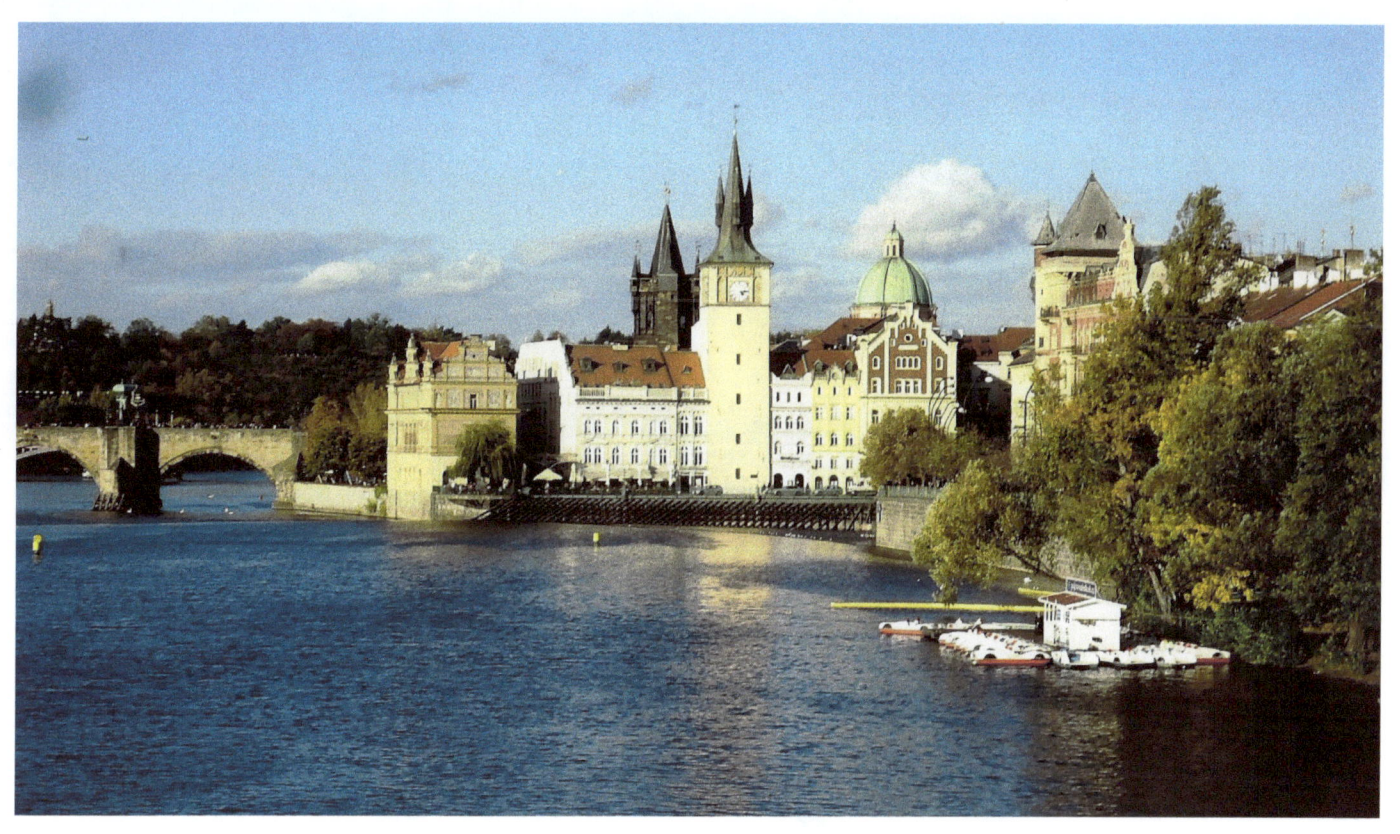

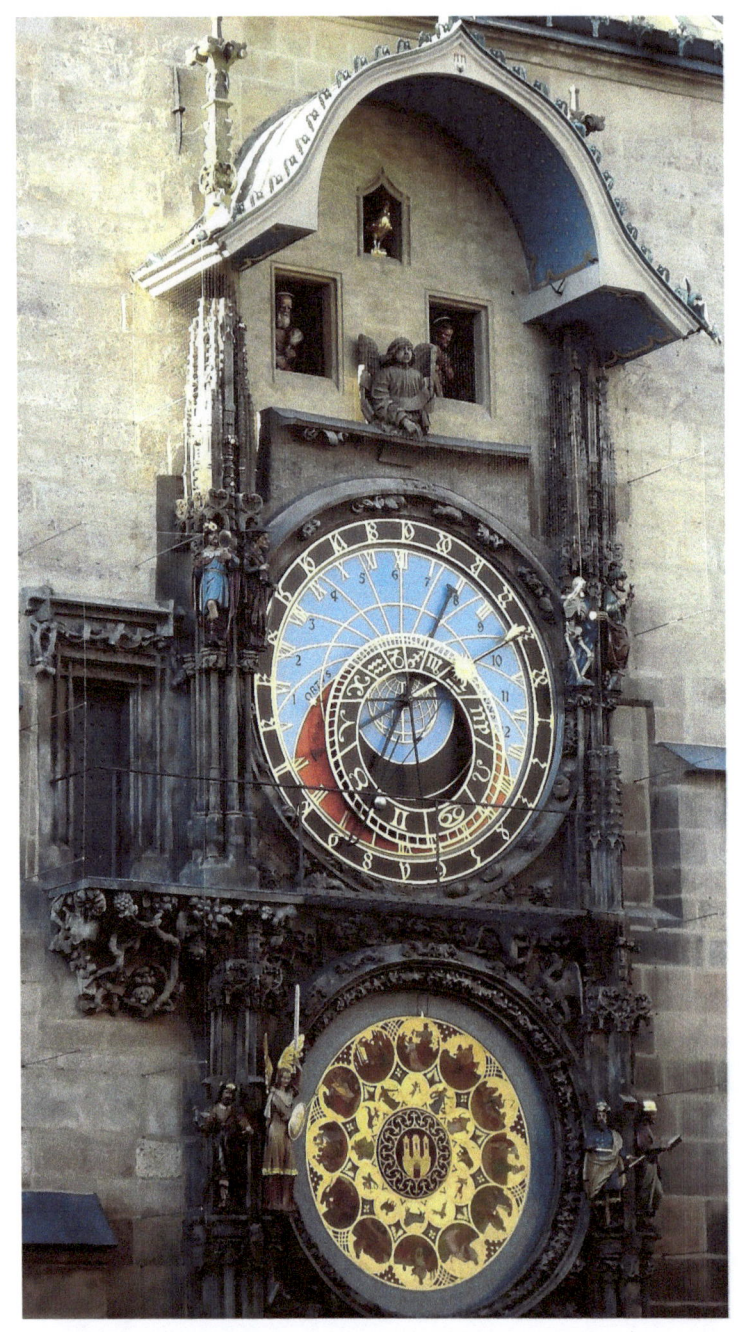

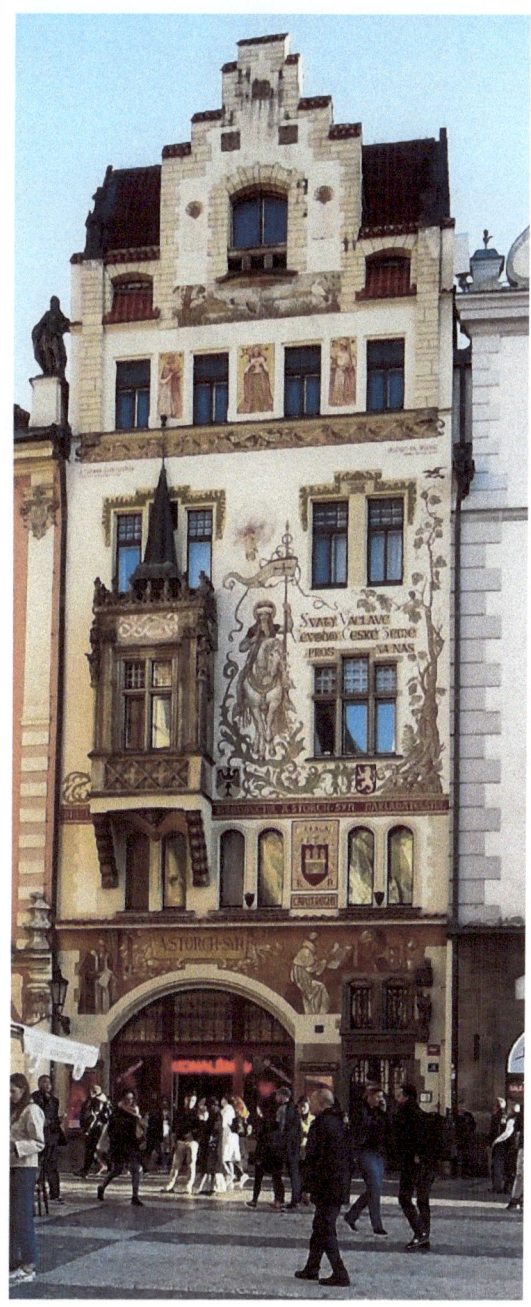

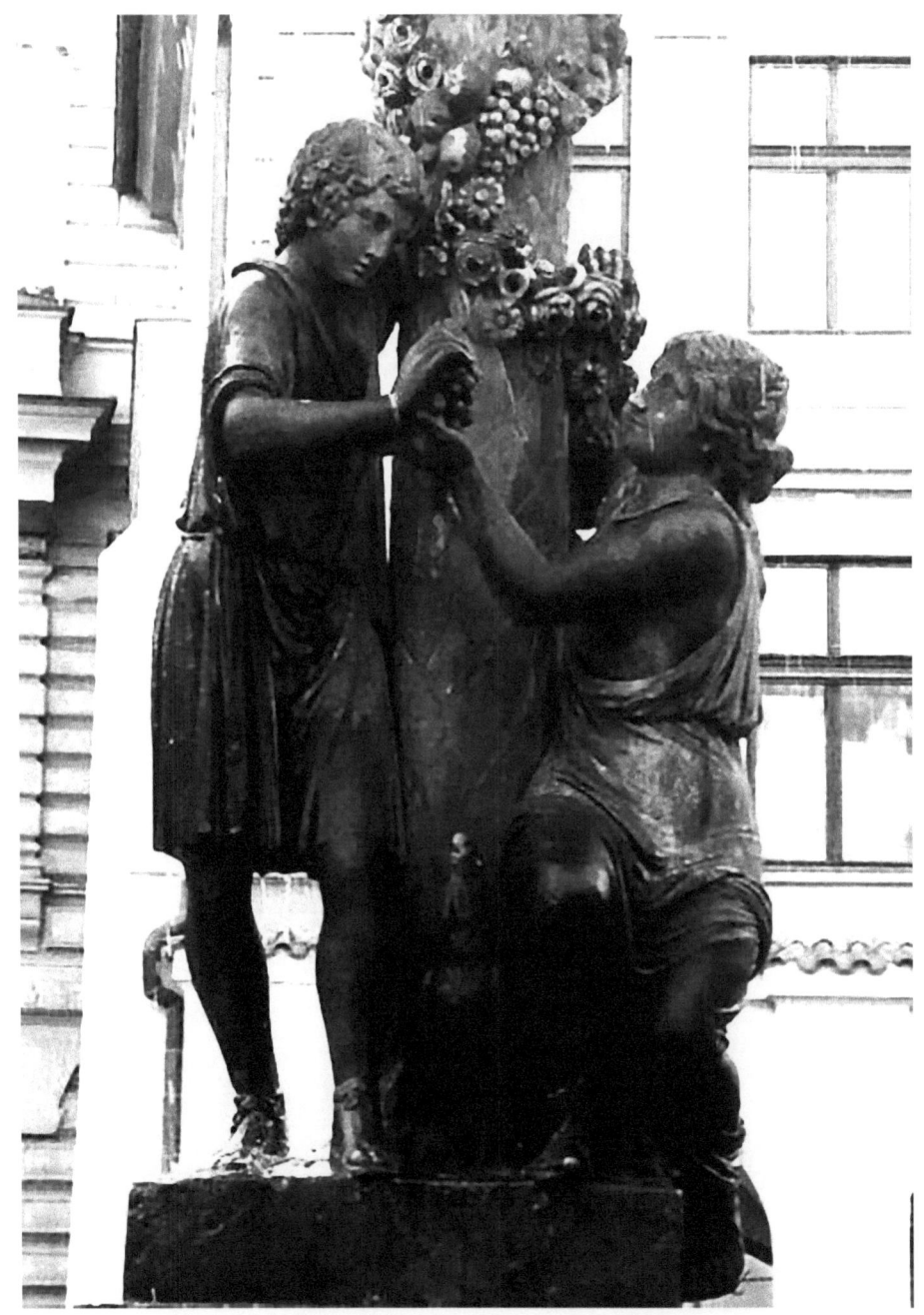

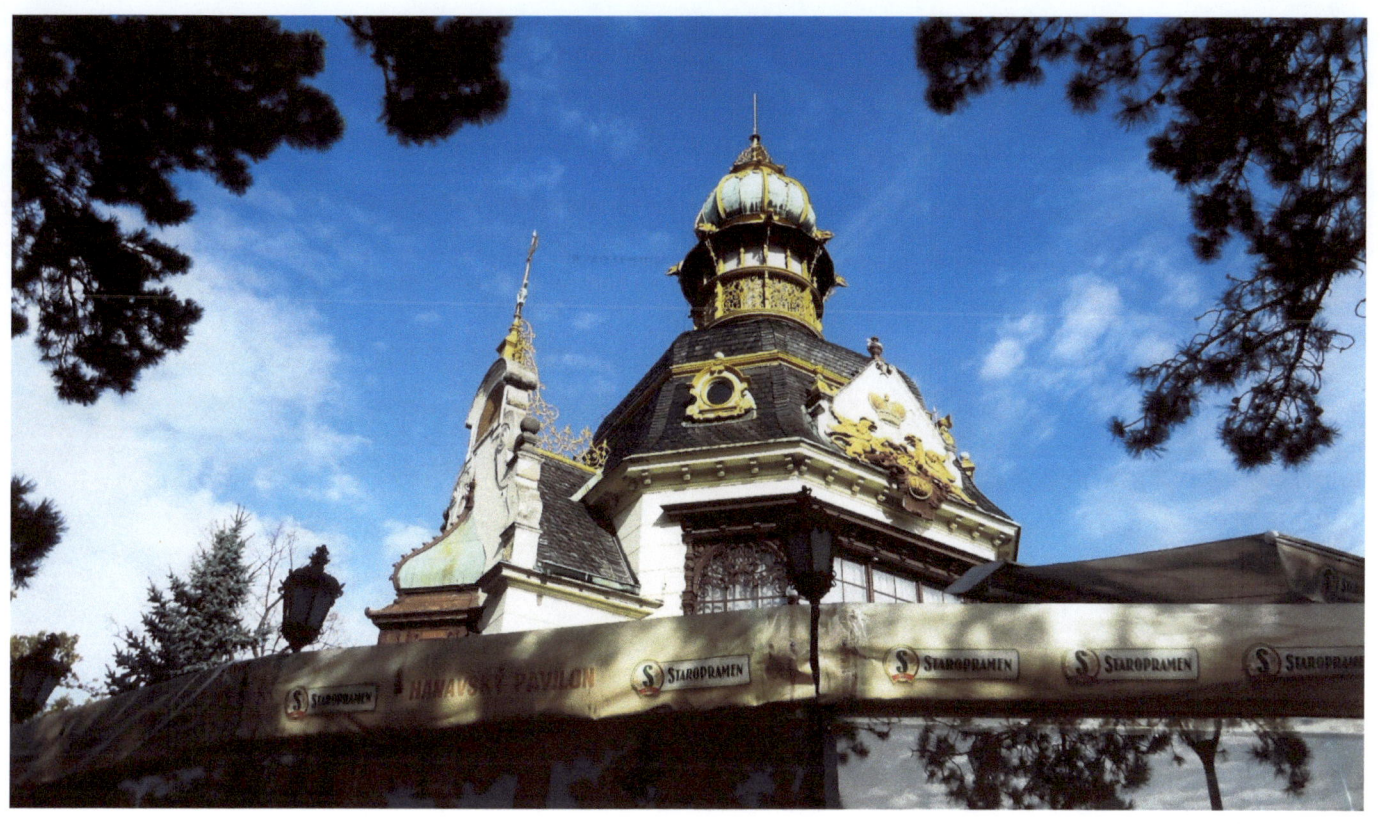

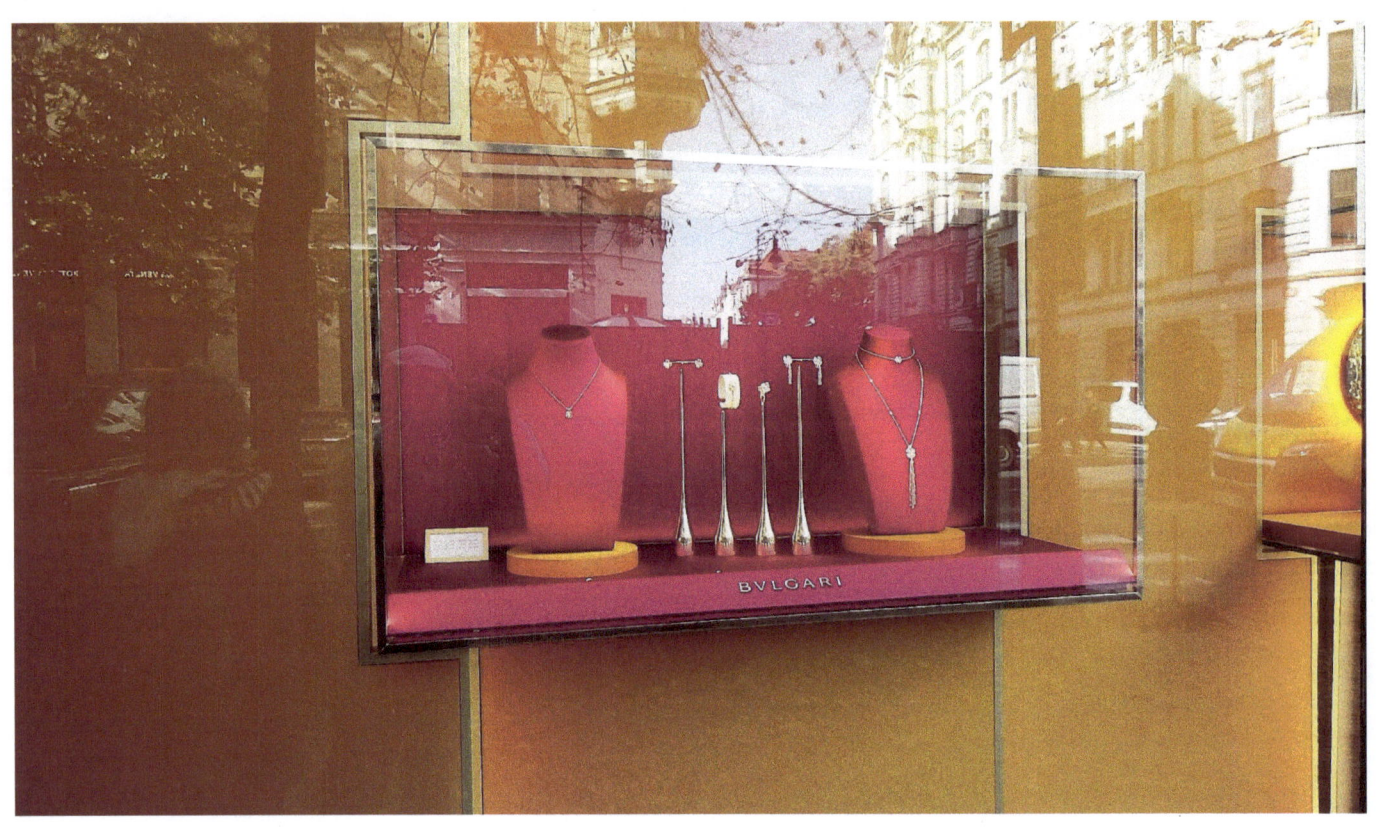

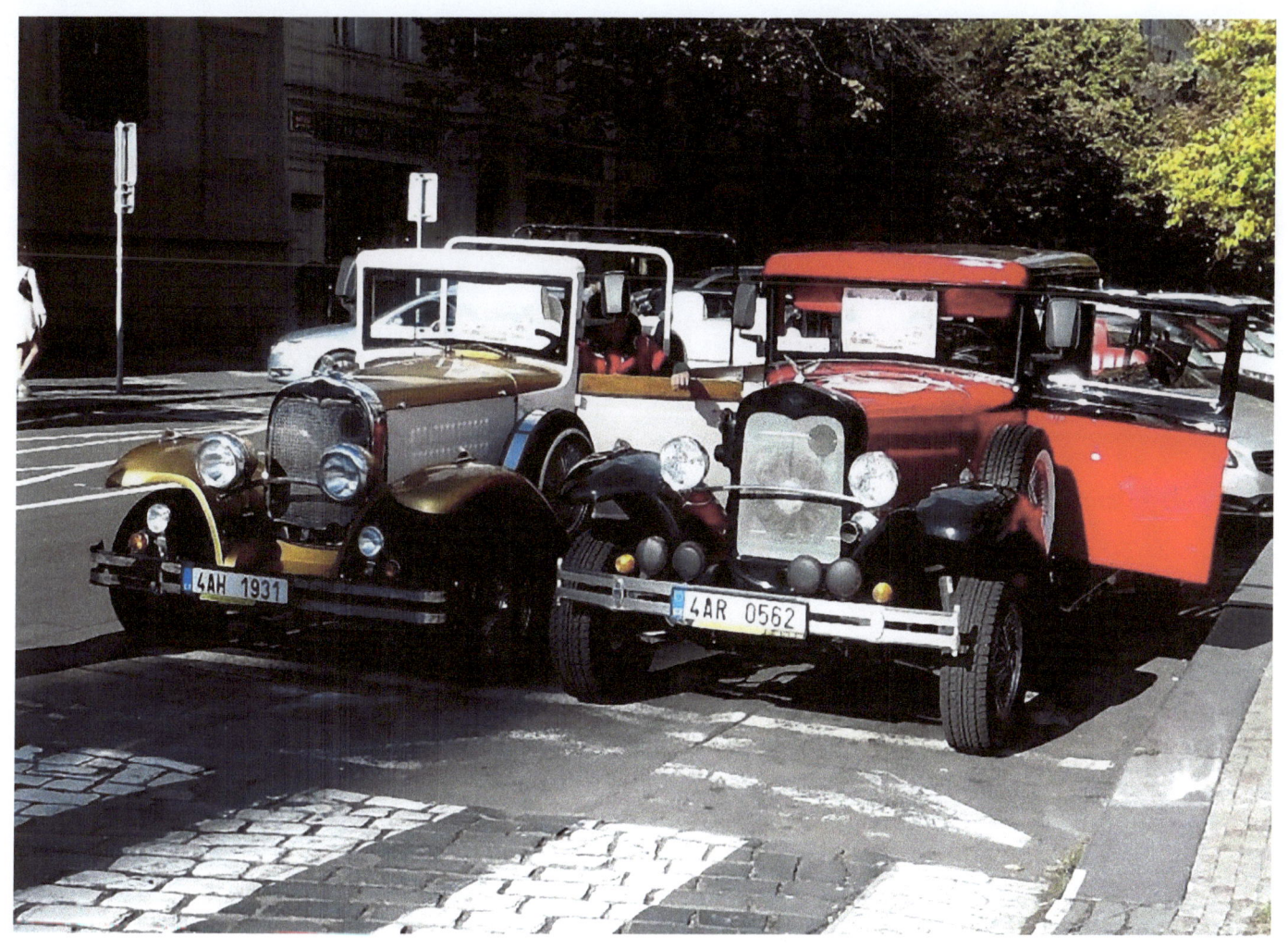

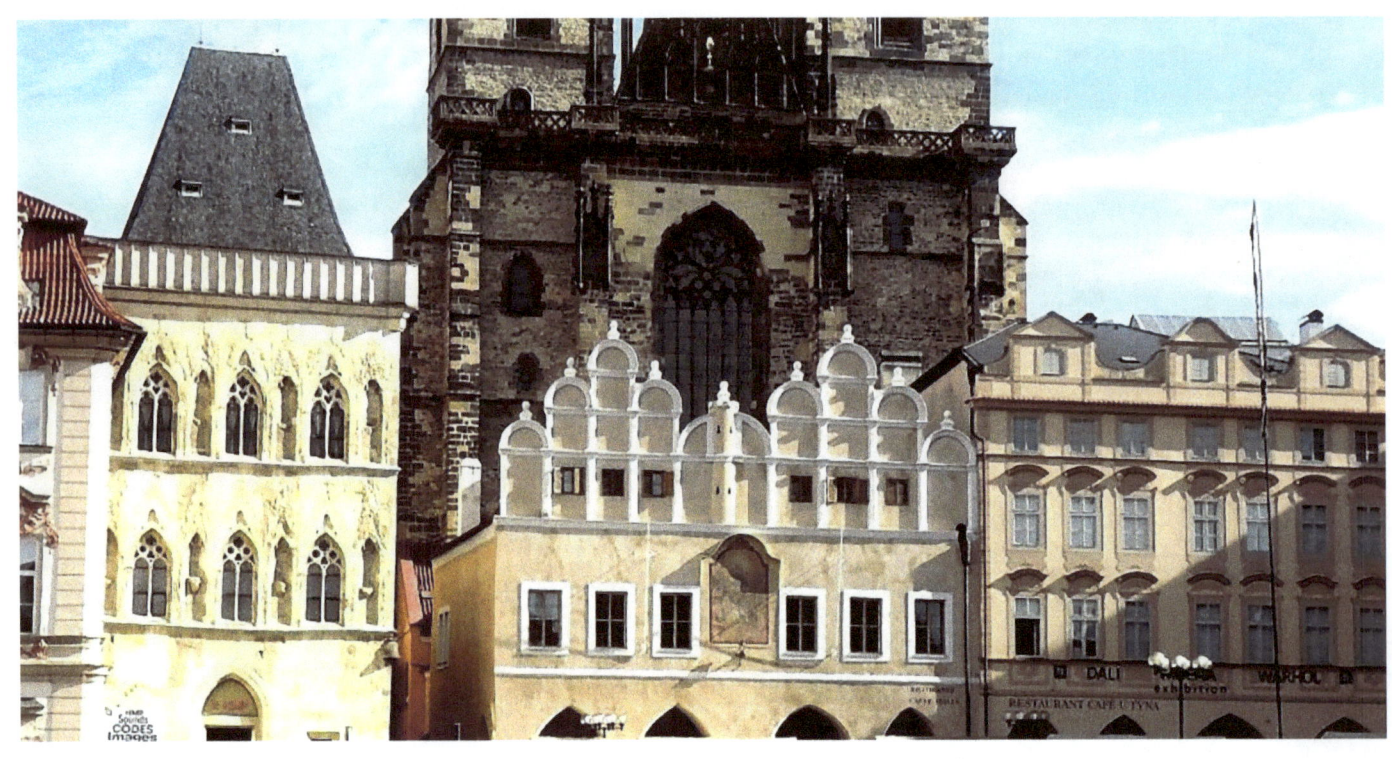

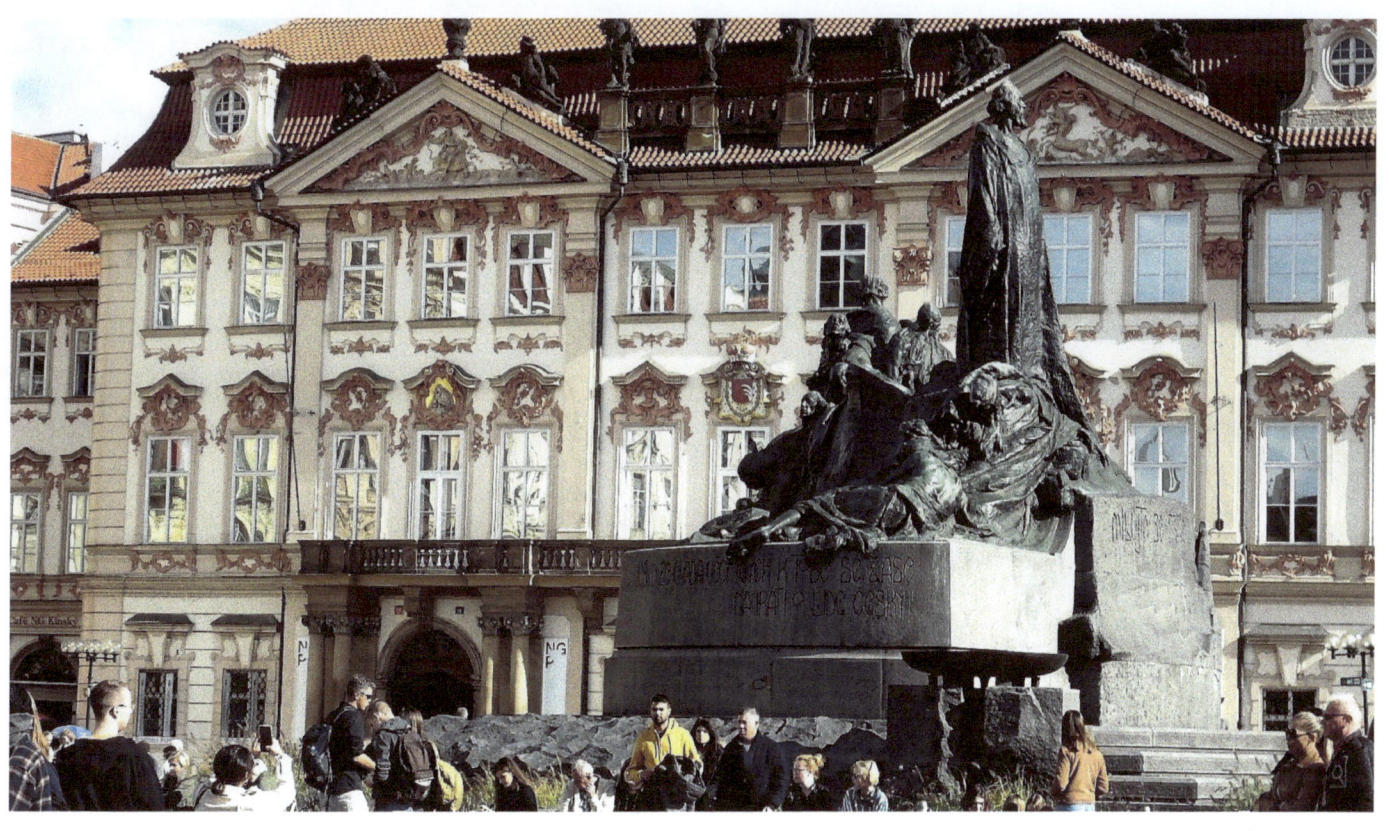

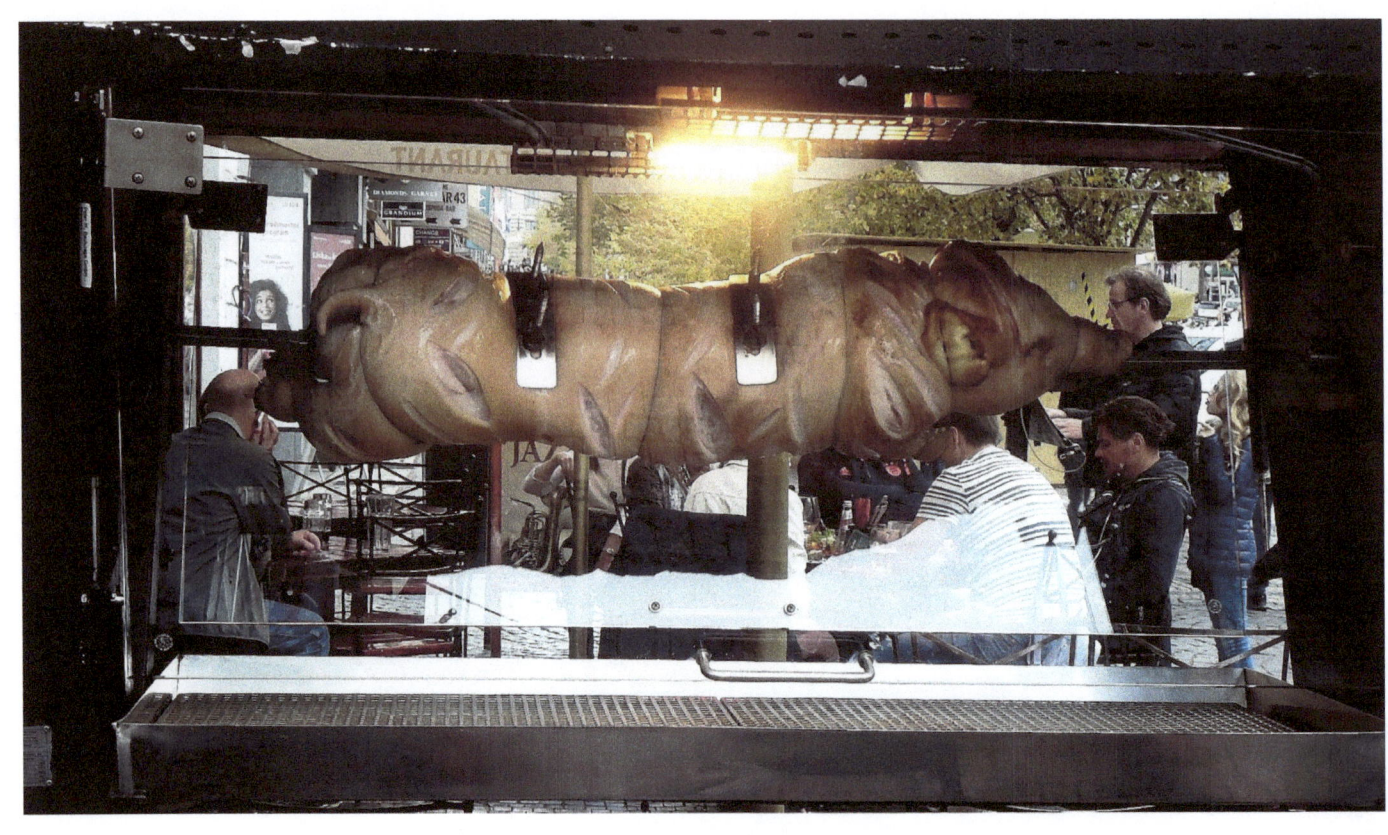

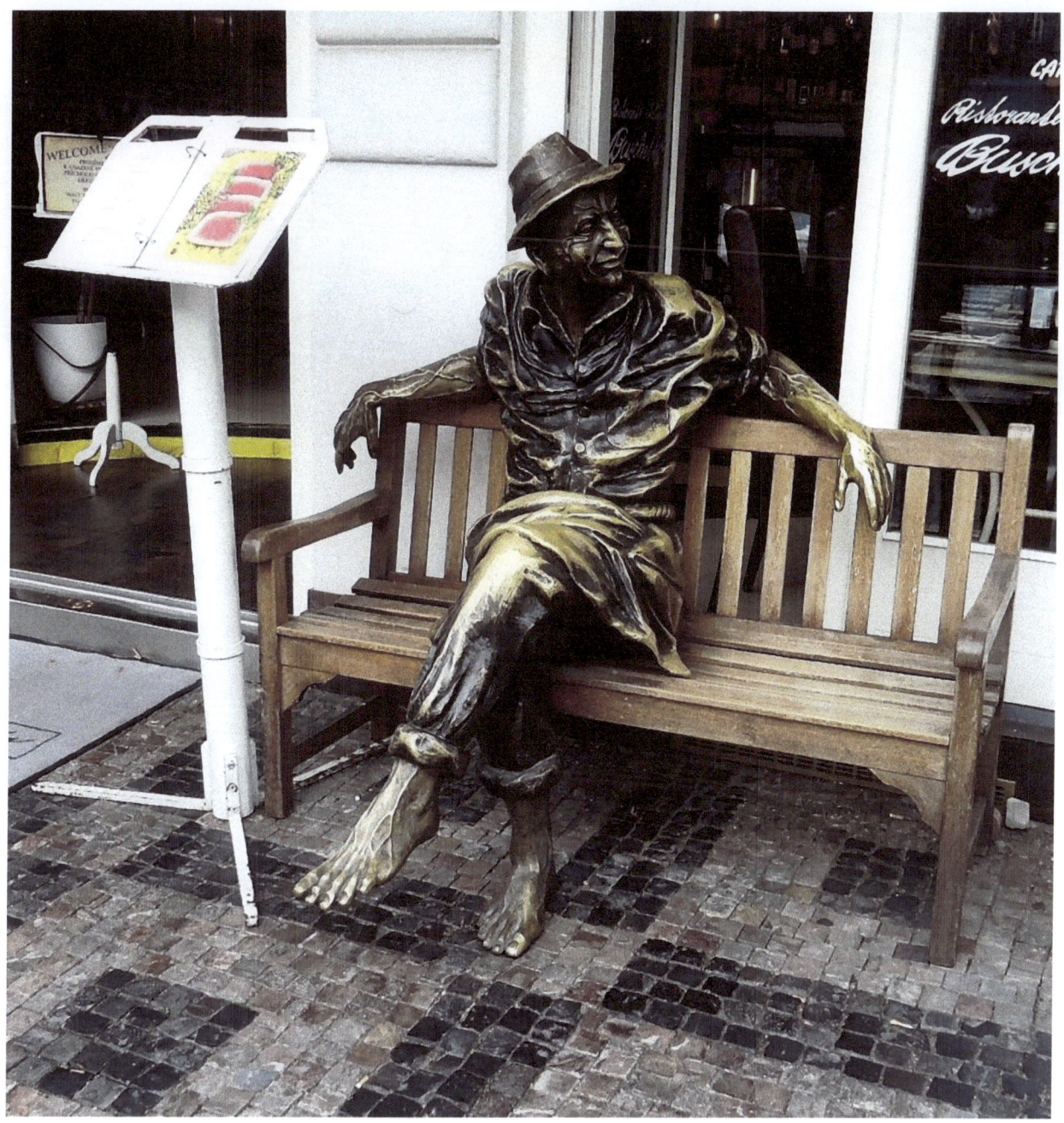

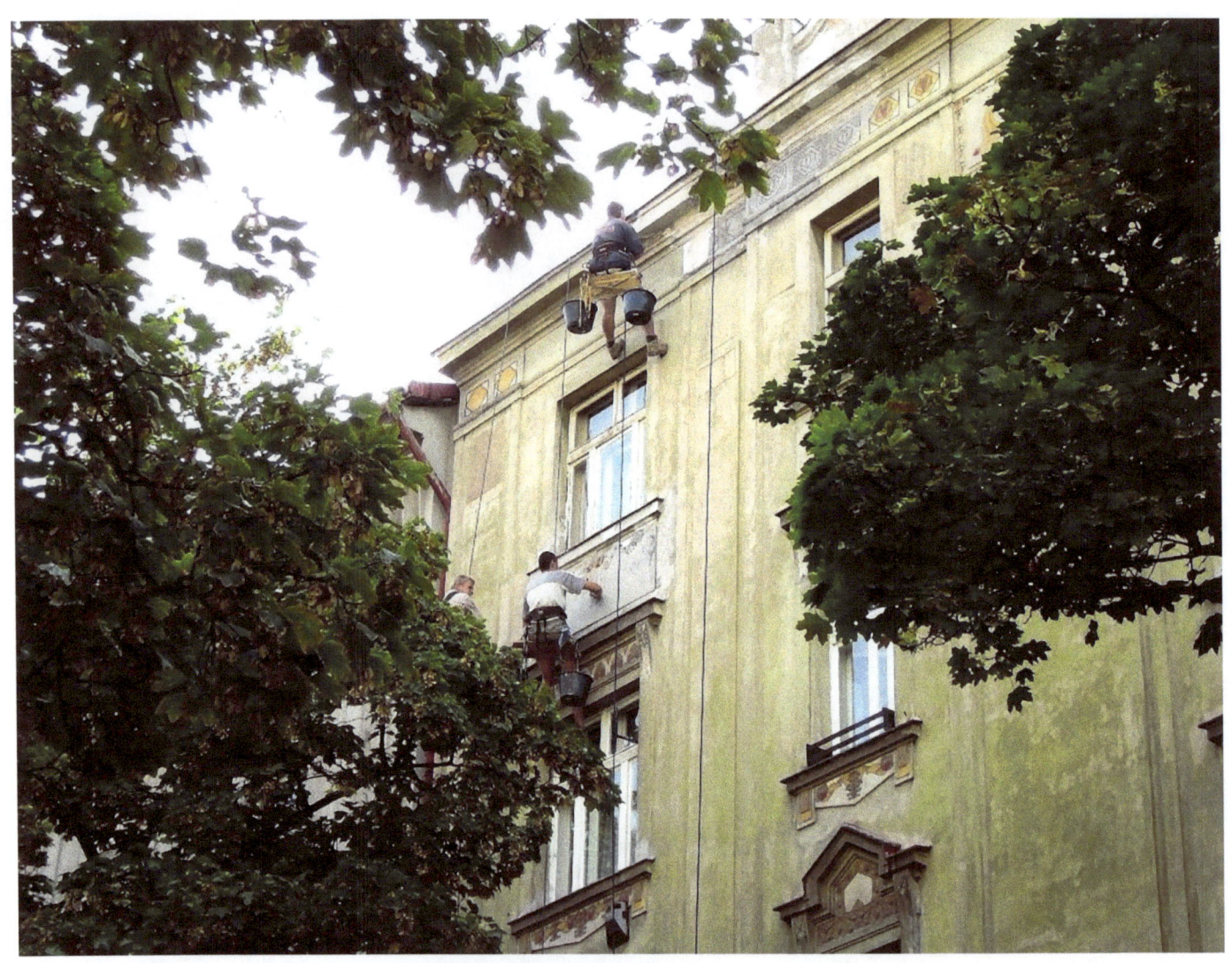

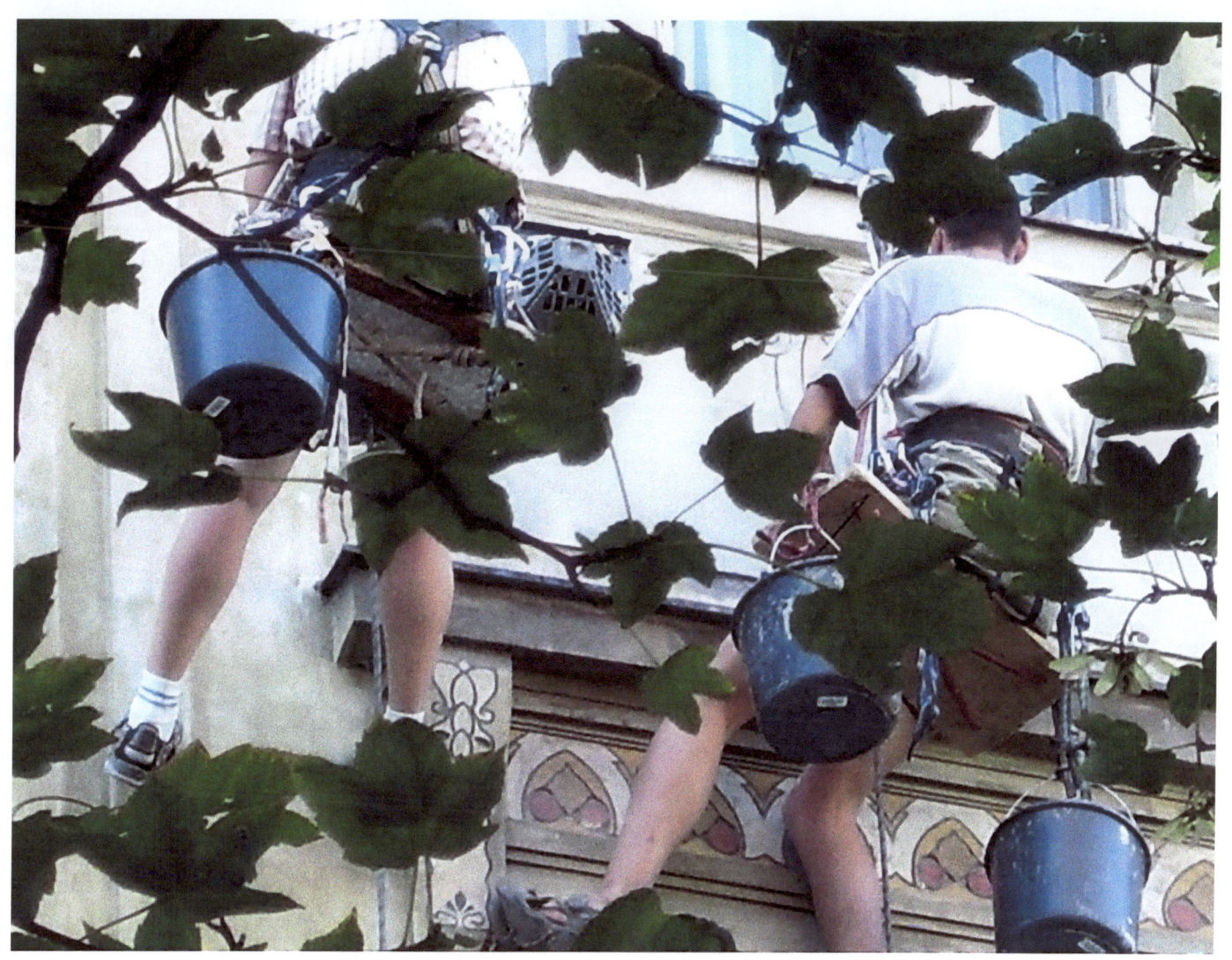

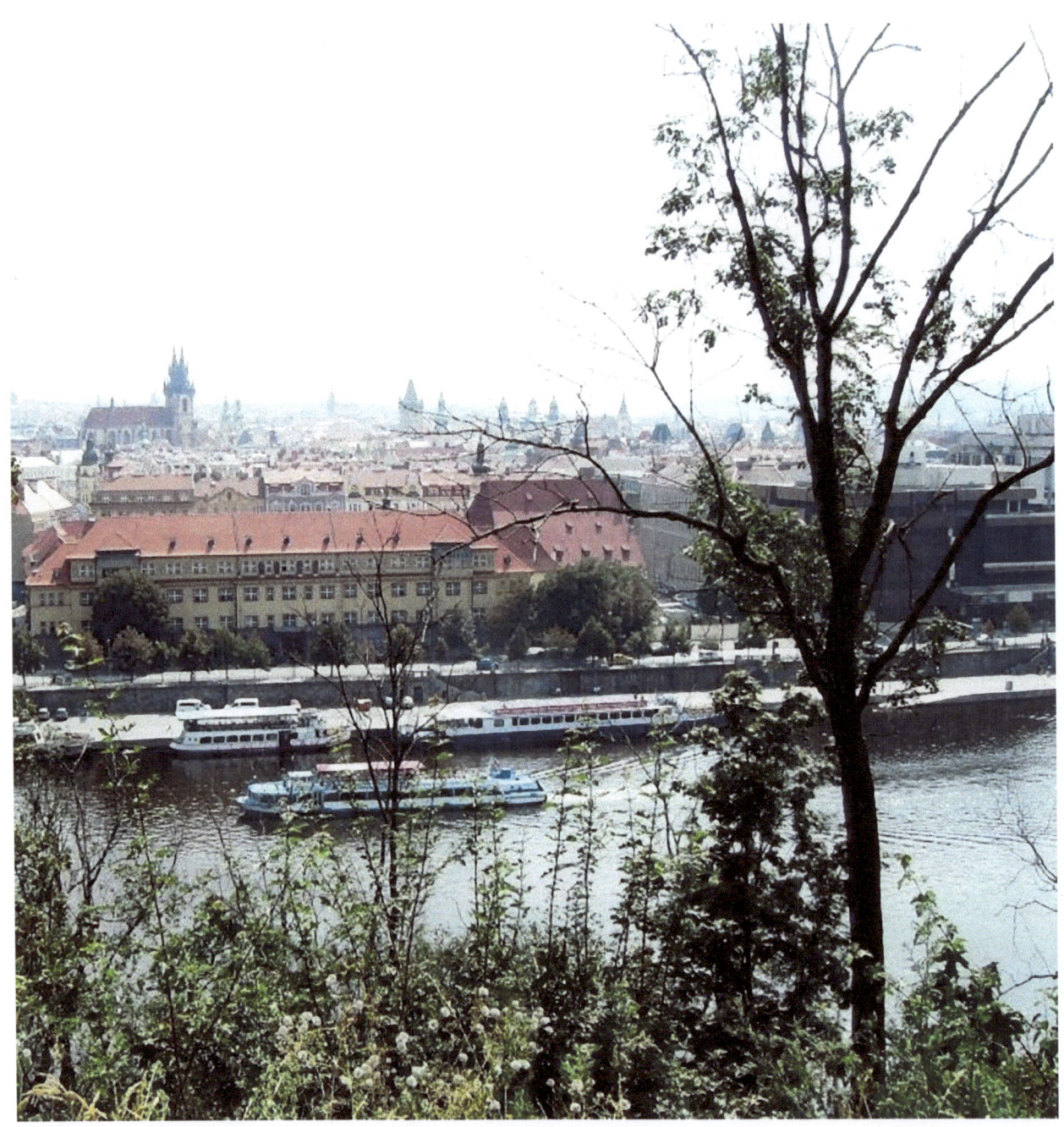

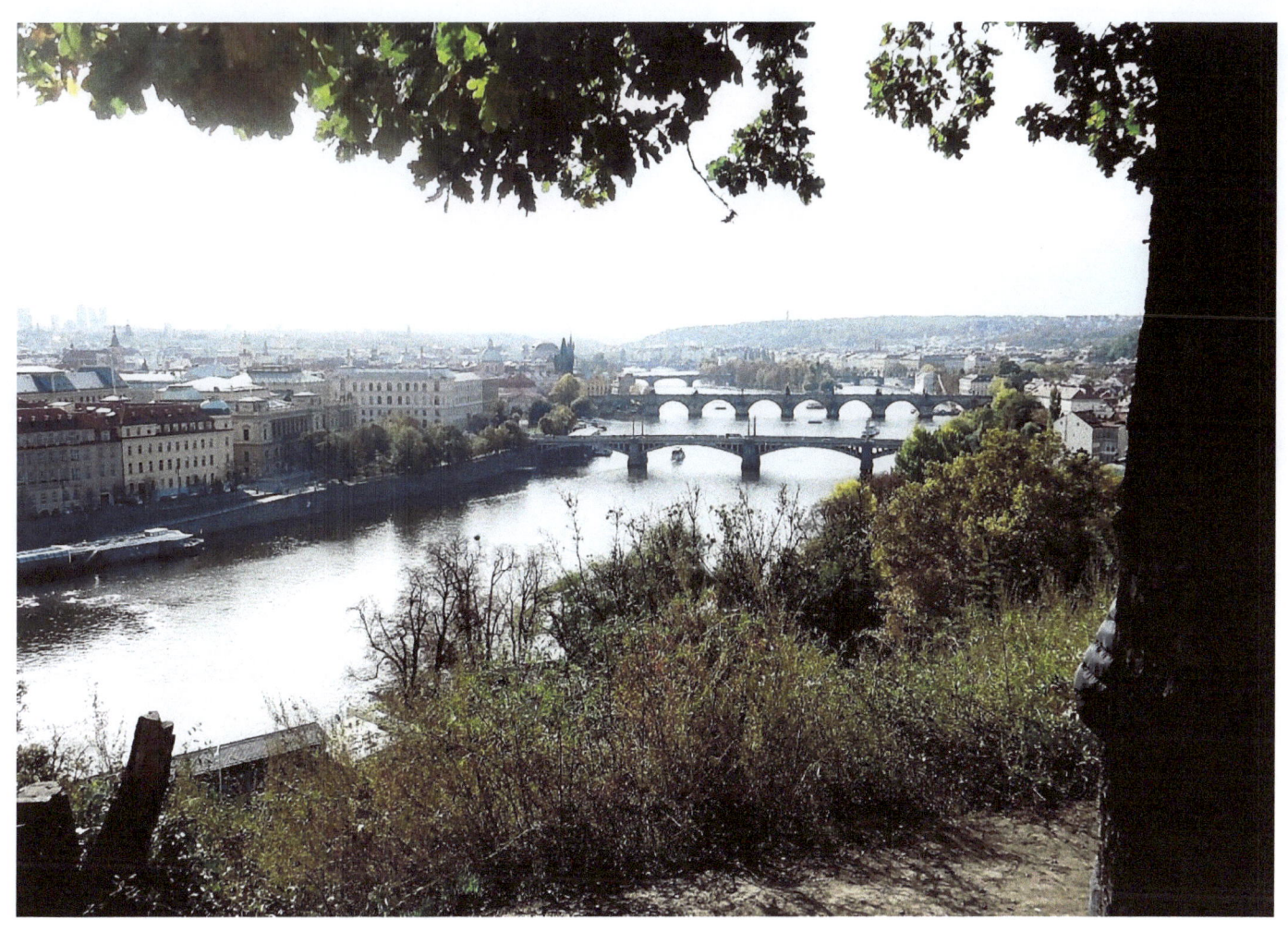

www.ingramcontent.com/pod-product-compliance
Lightning Source LLC
Chambersburg PA
CBHW051211220526
45473CB00003B/995